# EMPOWERED LEADERSHIP

KRIS PITTA

Copyright © 2020
KRIS PITTA
EMPOWERED LEADERSHIP
All rights reserved.

No part of this publication may be reproduced, distributed, or transmitted in any form or by any means, including photocopying, recording, or other electronic or mechanical methods, without the prior written permission of the publisher, except in the case of brief quotations embodied in critical reviews and certain other non-commercial uses permitted by copyright law.

KRIS PITTA

Printed in the United States of America
First Printing 2020
First Edition 2020

10 9 8 7 6 5 4 3 2 1

**To my parents:**
Thank you for encouraging me to dream big

**To my loving wife and children:**
Thank you for making my dreams come true

# Table of Contents

Introduction ............................................................................. 1
    The Dire Need for Effective Leaders ........................................ 1

**Chapter 1: The Art of Leadership** ................................................ 5
    What Is Leadership? ................................................................ 5
    Misconceptions Around Leadership ........................................ 8
    Evaluation of Positive Leadership ........................................... 12

**Chapter 2: Leadership, Power, or Both?** ................................... 22
    Power Without Leadership ..................................................... 22
    Leadership Without Power ..................................................... 24
    Leadership and Power ............................................................ 27
    The Wrong Winning Attitude ................................................ 32

**Chapter 3: Forms of Leadership Power** ..................................... 35
    Classification of Leadership Power ......................................... 35
    Factors Which Determine Leadership Power ........................ 45
    Winning Power ....................................................................... 50

**Chapter 4: Leadership Power and Personalities** ........................ 51
    Factors Which Dictate Types of Personalities ........................ 51
    Types of Personalities ............................................................. 56
    How Personalities Affect Leadership Power .......................... 60
    Managing Differences in Personalities ................................... 69

**Chapter 5: Leadership Styles Versus Leadership Power** ............. 71
    Leadership Styles .................................................................... 71
    Factors Affecting Leadership Styles ........................................ 99

The Mutual Influence Between Leadership Styles and Leadership Power .......... 103
Don't Fake It .......... 106
**Chapter 6: The Hidden Motive .......... 107**
Types of Motives .......... 107
Motives and Leadership Power .......... 116
**Chapter 7: The Influence in Leadership Power .......... 120**
Influence on Gender Bias .......... 120
Influence on the Vulnerable .......... 124
The Don'ts in Leadership Power .......... 127
**Chapter 8: A Winning Culture Cultivating Tool .......... 132**
A Culture of Mindful Listening .......... 132
Fostering Connectivity and Human Relationships .......... 139
**Chapter 9: Self-Awareness for Leaders .......... 143**
What is Self-Awareness? .......... 143
Is Self-Awareness Important? .......... 145
Types of Self-Awareness Tests .......... 147
**Conclusion .......... 160**
Task Orientation .......... 160
People Orientation .......... 162
The Action in "Not Doing" .......... 163

# Introduction

If there is one thing the world cannot afford to lose, it is leadership. After all, leadership brings a semblance of order, guidance, and direction where there might otherwise be nothing but chaos. However, just any leadership is not enough. The world needs authentic leadership that reinforces growth in both individuals and teams through creative inspiration. Moreover, the world is in dire need of leaders who are ethically dedicated to creating more copies of themselves to lead us in the future. After all, the trust that these leaders' team members bestow upon them should always be held in high esteem and empathetic conscience. Because, ultimately, misused leadership power is likely to only produce more leaders who do the same.

## The Dire Need for Effective Leaders

Team leadership is a serious responsibility that entails leaving the success of a group of people in the hands of one individual. This success extends to the self-esteem, feelings, and emotions of one's team members as well – not just their outward accomplishments. And even though failure is not always the leader's fault, the power embedded in leadership will always make it appear as if the leader could have done something different. In fact, to a certain extent, leadership makes omnipresence a reality by utilizing delegation and effective communication. That's why it can be incredibly detrimental when a leader is unaware of how to make the most productive use of their power.

Informed utilization of leadership power is a dynamic tool that has the potential to inspire even the most discouraged team. With enough effort, it can help mold a team culture that doesn't see losing or surrendering as viable options. Instead, they approach every problem primed to win. However, a leader must be aware of the factors affecting the proper use of his or her power. At the same time, they need to be properly informed of the "dos" and "don'ts" involved in exercising that power. In this book, leaders will find a manual with which they can sow a very important seed – one that helps grow a culture of leadership that authenticates winning while encouraging team members to plant seeds of their own.

## *Why We Need a Successful Leader for the Winning Team*

Under poor leadership, both teams and individuals can miss their moments to bloom, even when they have endless potential. Perhaps more depressing is that their explanation for their failures is not far-fetched. Perhaps their leader did not fully utilize his or her power, or – worse – overused or even misused it. After all, the very same power that can form a ladder to climb to success is also perfectly capable of derailing a team's efforts and throwing them back down.

Indeed, there is a wide range of reasons why a team, or simply individual members, might envy the team next door. One of the primary reasons is the type of spirit imparted to them by their leaders. A team leader who declares failing a possible option or who enforces winning by instilling fear, draining self-confidence, or curbing open-mindedness in their team members, only creates a "team" of failures and quitters. And with the rapidly increasing global competition most industries now face, quitters will be knocked down with little effort. This is why every leader must do their best to cultivate a winning attitude while also attempting to replicate their best qualities via mentoring.

It's worth remembering that leaders are always being appraised, especially by the people they lead. But people are not just out there looking for leaders to blame - they're also looking for leaders to commend. Still, there must be something to applaud. And with effective leadership, a winning mentality, and calculated, relevant, effective use of one's leadership power, a leader can maximize their chances of earning that applause. As it is the goal and pleasure of every great leader to see their followers ascend the ladder they create, they are always more than happy to replace a missing rung to keep their team going. They often imagine the type of future leaders they are creating – all the while knowing that the world will surely be a better place after their leading days are done.

## *Be the Responsible Leader*

Above all, being a responsible leader involves accepting accountability, be it social, economic, financial, emotional, or even political. An accountable leader values the sacredness of humanity and all the meaningful relationships that life necessitates. As tasks are accomplished and goals are met, these leaders must ultimately recognize that the sanctity of society should also be upheld at all costs. Responsibility entails doing whatever it takes to deliver high-quality services, which - in this case - is cultivating a winning spirit in both your team and yourself.

Every responsible leader will require information that can help them identify their "gray areas" so that they can make efforts to improve them. This goes hand in hand with other forms of continuous learning, which are essential to keeping pace with today's rapidly-changing professional landscape and the ever-evolving needs of one's team. Indeed, great leaders always have something to learn. In a famous quote, President John Quincy Adam's perfectly embodies the concept, saying that, "if your actions inspire others to dream more, learn more, do more, and become more, you are a leader.[1]" Ultimately, you need to be responsible for your success and for the success of those you lead. And don't wait for the metaphorical trumpet to blow before you start – the time to seize your leadership role is now! We'll start by exploring leadership as an art form and analyzing the creativity involved in leading both effectively and properly.

---

[1] *Qualtrics. (2020, May 20). 10 powerful quotes on leadership for your organization.* https://www.qualtrics.com/blog/10-powerful-leadership-quotes/

# Chapter 1: The Art of Leadership

Countries, communities, organizations, and even families all have some form of leadership in place. Indeed, leadership is a primary characteristic of groups, no matter how big or small they might be. However, there are misconceptions concerning just what leadership is. For example, positions, wealth, money, and power are usually misinterpreted as qualities that contribute to good leadership. Yet, there are countless examples of people who have these qualities but lack good leadership skills. In this chapter, I'll attempt to explore leadership as an art form - one that requires remarkable creativity on the leader's part in order to achieve the desired results.

## What Is Leadership?

Leadership is more than an influential position. Instead, it is a progressive process[2] where a leader develops the necessary qualities to guide and direct themselves and others while continually improving themselves through life's tests. This process also includes the gradual acceptance of the responsibility associated with their role. Of course, reducing a leader's power should always remain an option that team members can choose to exercise if

---

[2] Hughes, R. L.. (1993). *Leadership: Enhancing the lessons of experience.* ERIC. https://eric.ed.gov/?id=ED363927

current leadership fails to inspire a winning culture. To that point, it should be clear that the inability to resist leadership, for any reason, should not be interpreted as acceptance of that leadership. Also, for purposes of this chapter, I will attempt to describe leadership in two ways: these are either "passive and remote" or "active and involved."

## *Passive and Remote Leadership*

When leadership is implemented in an uninvolved manner, it is passive and remote. In such cases, the leader partially or fully abandons the procedures involved in completing assigned work - instead relegating it to their lower-ranking colleagues. This form of leadership is less connective and more neglective to the team members, which can often overwhelm them with duties that are not in their power to accomplish. In other words, the team is forced to invest valuable effort in trying to accomplish something that could have been done more easily had the leader been involved. When remote leadership is exercised, it is more likely that the leader will leave their followers' welfare, security, and emotional well-being unattended[3], leading to depletion of will, zeal, and performance in the team members. When under the direction of a passive leader, team players will be less motivated, which hinders the development of a winning culture. And, as there will be limited

---

[3] Barling, J., & Frone, M. R. (2016). *If only my leader would just do something! Passive leadership undermines employee well-being through role stressors and psychological resource depletion.* Stress and Health, 33(3), 211–222. https://doi.org/10.1002/smi.2697

connection and coordination between the leader and team, ambiguity can become the order of the day.

## *Active and Involved Leadership*

Active and involved leadership can significantly increase the likelihood of winning. This increase applies to both the team at large and each individual team member. By "involved" leadership, we are attempting to describe a leader who is focused on accomplishing tasks personally while being simultaneously committed to motivating their team. The end result of accomplishing a "win" is as essential to an active leader as the team's well-being and motivation. Involved and active leaders take a vastly different approach to their duties than those that are passive and remote. For instance, they know a good leader doesn't micromanage but instead has "micro interest." This means understanding the details of their projects and the process at work without making each team member feel as if they are under scrutiny.

An active leader is not fond of saying, "Do as I say and not as I do.[4]" Such a winning attitude in a leader can foster a culture of victory in the rest of the team, ultimately raising their enthusiasm about their achievements. Another characteristic of active leaders is their tendency to assume "role model" and "mentor" roles to their team members. They often accomplish this by being involved in daily activities and decision making. But apart from the indirect encouragement that stems from their involvement, an active leader

---

[4] *Selden, J. (1892). The table talk of John Selden. Clarendon Press.*

also takes care to verbally encourage team members, which can greatly contribute to their individual self-confidence. Obviously, high self-esteem is a vital asset in team members when creating a winning culture is the goal. However, doing so would be impossible without direct effort on the part of a leader who "leads to win."

## Misconceptions Around Leadership

The very notion of leadership is awash with misconceptions, which can distort the effective and objective fulfillment of the role. This tends to happen when leadership is allowed to be defined by circumstances, situations, social views, and even emotions. However, as leadership is a process, it should not be coerced. Rather, it should be molded and strengthened through a variety of scenarios.

### *Soft- or Loud-Spoken?*

It is a common misconception that being soft-spoken is a sign of weakness or an innate inability to lead. However, there is no loud- or soft-spoken leadership, as a leader can display both good and bad leadership qualities irrespective of their speaking style. You see, leadership is neither aggression nor silence, but a creative art that exerts positive influence. Of course, being soft-spoken or loud does affect the type of leadership one exudes and may also impact one's ability to get things done. Ultimately, what is most important is the leader's ability to successfully complete tasks by inspiring team members and cultivating a winning culture.

## *Gender*

Although gender-based discrimination in leadership is decreasing, thus paving the way for more women in leadership roles, the process has been rather slow. Unfortunately, some communities and organizations still refuse to acknowledge the existence of female leadership, let alone its potential for success. This misconception is even more notable in political settings, where gender remains a notable vehicle for discrimination. More interestingly, another study showed that women often underrate themselves as unwilling to take up leadership positions even when allowed to do so[5]. This is not because those women do not want leadership positions, but because they are uncertain whether they will be heard, especially by their male colleagues.

However, some studies have reported that females outperform their male counterparts in terms of many leadership skills. These include communication, problem-solving, planning, and creative analysis.[6] Even so, a study carried out by Szymanska & Rubin in 2018 showed that male team members underrate their female leader's leadership abilities even when such skills are evident, often while hiding behind the banner of male leadership.

---

[5] *Butler, D. M., & Preece, J. R. (2016). Recruitment and perceptions of gender bias in party leader support. Political Research Quarterly, 69(4), 842–851.* *https://doi.org/10.1177/1065912916668412*

[6] *Colantuono, S. (n.d.). What's changed in perceptions of women in leadership? Not much. Www.Leadingwomen.Biz.* *https://www.leadingwomen.biz/blog/bid/70211/what-s-changed-for-women-in-leadership-not-much*

Of course, such gender-based misperceptions are a double-edged sword when it comes to leadership. This is because many people interpret male leadership as aggressive and self-centered, which is not always the case. Nevertheless, the mindset is quite pervasive among female team members who can recall one or more difficult experiences that took place under a man's leadership. Alternatively, some women are primed to interpret male leadership this way via second-hand testimonials from other women. Ultimately, it is important to note that when measured based on gender affiliation, any assessment of leadership ability is bound to be misleading.

## *Titles*

Information related to the link between titles and leadership is often distorted, and therefore frequently misunderstood. But can either of the two exist without the other?

### Title Without Leadership

A title on its own is not leadership, nor does it confer it. A title merely provides a person with positional influence, which can only be made worthwhile when combined with authentic leadership skills. You see, in the modern world, leadership is measured via output, not the possession of a crown. It is what a leader does after a title is bestowed on him that matters most. Will they be able to create an environment that is conducive to inspiration, growth, and success? If the answer is no, the title is virtually meaningless.

## Leadership Without a Title

It is possible – even common – for an individual to exhibit excellent leadership qualities without a title. Moreover, should a title be bestowed upon an individual because of the leadership qualities they have demonstrated, that title becomes a confirmation of their ability to lead. As I've already discussed, those leaders who lead "from within" are often more concerned about making a positive impact than their current title.

Let's examine the story of Isis Johnson, who started the Isis Johnson Foundation. Triggered by seeing a visual of Ethiopian children starving, four-year-old Isis began a charity organization using only two things: left-over chicken and leadership qualities. Gradually, she began collecting food donations for hungry children in her community, and later she became a contact point for many well-established donors. However, her title, "Founder," only came later in response to the leadership qualities she exhibited.[7]

## Title and Leadership

While a title is not leadership, it is important to note that it is not irrelevant in leadership. After all, a title can confer a positional advantage to a leader, thus enhancing their ability to exercise their leadership qualities. There are cases where it would be difficult – even impossible – to make a leadership impact without a title, regardless of how exceptional one's abilities might be. In such cases,

---

[7] Salcedo, M. (2016, May 1). *Stone soup for the soul. Inquirer.Net.*
*https://business.inquirer.net/209944/stone-soup-for-the-soul*

a title becomes an asset to leadership. Indeed, influencing an organization's top brass would be quite a challenge without a title. After all, it is that title that allows you to be part of the organization's executive meetings and decision-making sessions. Moreover, being assigned a universally-respected title might increase the chances of your team members listening to you. According to John Maxwell (Lead From Where You Are, 2010), you can lead without title by developing strong relationships with key people, defining the "win" in terms of teamwork, engaging in continual communication, and accepting the responsibility of being an informal leader.

## Evaluation of Positive Leadership

Like most attributes, leadership can be assessed and evaluated in order to determine its viability or success. In fact, evaluating leadership is essential to the proper function of team members, organizations, communities, countries, and the leaders themselves. In this book, I describe positive leadership as both people and task-oriented. I also highlight it as the ability to inspire a winning attitude in team members, provide constructive feedback, and perform assertive conflict resolution.

One can evaluate leadership by both qualitative and quantitative means. In a quantitative evaluation, the goal is to summarize the leader's accomplishments into a numerical value. Alternatively, a qualitative assessment attempts to measure the non-numerical aspects of leadership. Such analysis relies on the procurement of data via yes/no, true/false, and present/absent questions, whose answers range from "highly agree" to "neutral" to "highly disagree."

In essence, qualitative leadership can be described as evaluating what a leader does in order to deliver results. We will discuss this measurement method in detail later in this chapter.

## *Evaluation According to Leadership Efforts*

Precisely what a leader does in delivering their guidance is essential to the success of his or her team. It is these efforts that both establish and improve their approach to leadership. To that point, it is crucial to remember that what a leader does and how they do it are equally important.

### Communication Approach and Skills

Perhaps you've heard of the 7-38-55 rule of communication? It refers to a study that determined that 7% of any message is communicated through spoken words, 38% through tone of voice, and 55% through body language (Silent Messages, Mehrabian). Obviously, this suggests that body language doesn't just play an important role in communication, but a dominant one.

Of course, all relevant communication, when implemented correctly, is an effective tool for positive leaders. And by communication, we're referring to the process whereby any form of an encoded message is transmitted by the sender, through the relevant medium, to the receiver, who decodes and interprets it before giving feedback.[8] Obviously, we know that communication

---

[8] *Directing communication. (2019, July 12). Toppr-Guides.*
https://www.toppr.com/guides/business-studies/directing/communication/

is a critical tool for conveying information in a two-way format. However, a leader needs to know how to communicate and relay messages properly, thereby ensuring his or her messages are interpreted correctly. Whether or not the interpretation was correct or not, can be determined by feedback.

Messages can be relayed through body language, text, silence, or spoken word. Body language and silence[9] are part of the communication process, as they can both send interpretable messages. Furthermore, gestures, postures, the distance between speakers, smiling, and eye contact are all forms of non-verbal communication, as they, too, send messages without using spoken or written words.[10] Non-verbal communication is actually considered the sincerest form of communication.

This is because when verbal and non-verbal communication is ambiguous, both can be easily misinterpreted[11]

According to Stephen Covey, most people do not listen with the intent to understand. Instead, they listen with the intent to reply. This highlights the importance of active listening skills in communication. Taking that into account, there are four communication styles that we can identify in humans. They are

---

[9] Drucker, P. F. (2017). *The analytic situation: How patient and therapist communicate.* Routledge.

[10] Nordquist, R. (2019). What is nonverbal communication? ThoughtCo. https://www.thoughtco.com/what-is-nonverbal-communication-1691351

[11] Goleman, D. (1991, September 17). Non-verbal cues are easy to misinterpret. The New York Times. https://www.nytimes.com/1991/09/17/science/non-verbal-cues-are-easy-to-misinterpret.html

Doer, Thinker, Influencer, and Connector. The Doers tend to be high achievers and leaders that drive necessary results. However, they also tend to be impatient and insensitive to others. When you communicate with Doers, you have to be clear, specific, and to the point, as they tend only to discuss work. They will also typically ask for the basis for your ideas in order to evaluate their merit.

The Influencers can lighten up any room, even in the darkest moments. They are inspirational, encouraging, and understanding. However, their decision-making skills can often seem impractical. Moreover, they tend to procrastinate on assignments they do not like. When you communicate with Influencers, you need to provide a warm and friendly environment and be sure to show you care. They typically don't like to deal with many details, so it often helps to put such details in writing. At the same time, they dislike it when team members don't let them talk or ask about facts and figures.

The Connectors are reliable team players who look after everyone on their team. That said, they can also be non-supportive of bossy people. When you communicate with Connectors, it's best to begin with a personal comment to break the ice. After that, present your case efficiently in a clear and non-threatening way. Remember, these individuals do not like it when team members force them to respond quickly or demand abrupt change.

The Thinkers tend to excel when they like their work and can think through all angles and contingencies effectively. However, they can sometimes appear combative, critical, and sarcastic. When you communicate with Thinkers, you need to prepare in advance and brace yourself for a debate. These individuals tend to appreciate colleagues who are accurate and realistic. They do not like team members that are disorganized or approach them with unrealistic deadlines.

Understanding the nitty-gritty of communication styles can help leaders effectively interpret messages from their teams. This can prove essential to minimizing the sort of understandings that hinder progress and hamper proper teamwork. Effective communication can get things done, and getting things done can help lead to more effective communication. To that point, the quality of one's leadership can always be evaluated on how effectively they communicate.

## Continuous Learning

Figure 1: Continuous learning is key.

Alvin Toffler said, "the illiterate of the 21st century will not be those who cannot read and write, but those who cannot learn, unlearn and relearn.¹²" Indeed, the literacy of the modern era is the ability to learn new things and repeat those learning processes when necessary. After all, leadership without continuous learning will only result in redundancy. At the same time, it will be difficult to lead those who are keeping up with or even exceeding one's own learning processes.

An effective, positive leader needs to find opportunities to learn in everyday scenarios, particularly conflicts. Though conflicts are often viewed negatively, developing an attitude that encourages you to see conflicts as a learning opportunity can be extremely beneficial. A good example is learning to acknowledge and appreciate each party's differing views. This often takes this ability to truly appreciate others' thoughts and see your own thoughts from a different perspective. Additionally, the whole journey through a conflict can help a leader study the character, reactions, and attitudes of each of their team members up until the moment it is resolved. This is because we often unveil who we really are when subjected to stress.

Enrolling in an active learning session on leadership can have a rejuvenating effect on any leader. Fortunately, many such professional learning sessions are available online, allowing leaders to study without taking time away from their jobs. After all, the goal of the learning process is not to earn some certificate but to acquire the sort of leadership qualities that can only be imparted through knowledge. Of course, some leaders may still opt to enroll

---

[12] *TeachThought Staff. (2017, October 11). Top 50 best quotes about learning.* *https://www.teachthought.com/learning/52-best-quotes-about-learning/*

in full-time courses, which is perfectly fine, providing it is convenient for them.

Leaders that continuously learn are more likely to see an improvement in their decision-making abilities, how they engage with team members, their conflict resolution techniques, and their overall productivity. Also, by creating a "learning culture," they display the extent to which they will go to positively impact the people in their lives and career. Therefore, an analysis of a leader's ability to foster a learning culture is an essential qualitative evaluation method for determining that leader's commitment to success.

## *Evaluation According to the Impact of Leadership*

Every form of leadership has visible and invisible impacts on individual team members, the team at large, the organization, and the leaders themselves. Depending on whether these impacts are good or bad, one can extrapolate an overall positive or negative influence from the leader.

### Collective Goal Achievement by the Team

The achievement of set objectives and goals is a crucial leadership evaluation method. It highlights the leader's dedication to winning while also reflecting the quality of the team's winning culture. After all, when a team successfully

Figure 2: Collective goal achievement reflects positive leadership.

meets its targets, the team members become increasingly acquainted with winning and will display an interest in maintaining the victory-oriented habit. Indeed, the leader's efforts to inspire their team and create a group of "conquerors" can go a long way toward contributing to this.

Generally, team management skills will be reflected through the achievement of the team's collective targets. As the team achieves various goals, it reflects their leader's delegation skills and ability to foster involvement from all team members. And should the goals set by the leader and their team be far beyond the average, the team will be even more likely to develop an elevated sense of purpose. With such high expectations and sincere motivation, the team will be in a position to far exceed their goals.

Still, fostering a winning culture in a team means accommodating diversity in abilities, views, and personalities. Doing so requires a leader who is willing to engage with, understand, and grow along with their team members. In achieving team goals, the leader displays their ability to build and maintain relationships with team members, a hallmark of positive leadership.

## Individual Growth of Team Members

As the team achieves its goals, team members' individual goals are also met, and the growth of individual members of the team is promoted. Team member's professional growth is directly proportional to their growth in skills, knowledge, and attitudes.[13] These team member characteristics result from the emotional, social, and educational experiences they have in their work environments – environments created by their leaders.

Clearly, the involvement of team members in the execution of crucial tasks offers them practical opportunities for learning and development. These participant team members will nearly always develop a sense of responsibility and commitment as they contribute to the team's overall goals and the organization's overall mission. At the same time, talent identification among team members helps the leader determine who to delegate tasks to and where members might need improvement. Moreover, as they accomplish the team's collective goal, each team member's abilities are enhanced.

---

[13] *Mourão, L. (2018). The role of leadership in the professional development of subordinates. Leadership. https://doi.org/10.5772/intechopen.76056*

This individual growth reflects the leader's ability to motivate and encourage their subordinates as well as their ability to lead by example. Therefore, it's fair to say that individual team member growth and the leader's positive leadership skills are fundamentally interconnected.

# Chapter 2: Leadership, Power, or Both?

We call the potential influence wielded by an individual in a leadership position *leadership power*. In this chapter, I will delve deeper into the fundamentals of both aspects of this term, and how they can be combined. For instance, does a leader need both power and leadership ability to be a successful leader? How does each component contribute to their ability to instill a winning mentality in their team members? In the end, it is far more probably that each element has different implications for the applied methods in getting things done. This, in turn, has implications for the team's results.

## Power Without Leadership

It should go without saying that some people have power but lack the qualities of leadership. Power is quite simply defined as "the control that an individual or group has over others.[14]" We can separate power from leadership by remembering that power *controls* while leadership *influences*. Therefore, if one were to have power but no leadership, they would have control but no influence. This might cause them to attempt to gain influence through forceful acts, included violence. For our purposes, we can define violence as

---

[14] *Power. (n.d.). Merriam-Webster.Com.* https://www.merriam-webster.com/dictionary/power

the act of instilling fear in team members to force them to accomplish goals. Of course, when this happens, personal relationships are usually neglected.

Let's consider the example of a male hiring manager who requests sexual favors to hire a female applicant. This is a person imbued with plenty of power but who lacks a single iota of leadership. At the same time, this manager is also misusing his power. Now, let's assume the female applicant agrees to the manager's conditions and gets the job. She will now be far more likely to work in a state of fear. In this case, she fears that failing to maintain the hiring manager's immoral requirements might cause her to lose her job.

Clearly, while leadership without power can often work well, power without leadership skills can be disastrous, as it can be misused too easily. Moreover, as we'll see, some individuals who lack leadership but wield power may directly or indirectly attach leadership to that power.

## *Direct Attachment of Leadership to Power*

It is possible for individuals with power to develop leadership skills, but it often requires both willingness and effort on their part. Coupling power with leadership, specifically good leadership skills, can often temper the temptation to misuse that power. This is beneficial to everyone involved because while idle power is helpless, misused power is usually dangerous. For example, if we were to imagine power in terms of electricity, you might say that good leadership is the "surge protector" guarding against damage that can be caused by unchecked power.

Instead of instilling fear and forceful control to resolve conflicts, good leadership demands an individual apply assertiveness to conflict resolution. However, at the same time, it can also suggest the proper steps of doing so. Potential leaders can learn to do this as they go, through trial and error, or by closely observing a good leader of their choice. In organizations, one can typically find a mentor or sponsor who can easily fit into this role.

## *Indirect Attachment of Leadership to Power*

It's possible for powerful people who lack leadership qualities to still perform well. However, this is usually dependent on them surrounding themselves with individuals who have remarkable leadership acumen. Such colleagues can be positioned as advisors, counselors, or regulators who can offer opinions on the correct course of action. In this manner, power can be regulated and directed toward the proper goals. Moreover, having people with leadership qualities on hand might allow one to quickly learn the essential aspects of leadership through experience. In this case, good communication and networking abilities would be essential, as would an honest desire to surround oneself with the right people.

## Leadership Without Power

Leadership is usually viewed as hierarchical in that there must be a leader exerting power on team members. In that sense, power becomes a gravitational influence moving from the leader at the top toward the team members at the bottom. If this is the case, collaborations in which power is not exerted downward would no longer be vertical, but horizontal.

For our purposes, we refer to such a leadership model as "leadership without power" – a situation in which there are no influential positions attached to the leadership role.

## *Horizontal Leadership*

This leadership approach, also referred to as lateral leadership, is based on lateral thinking and analysis. The leader seeks the contribution of ideas, thoughts, and insights from all the team members.[15] This is far removed from a situation in which a leader might enact self-thought commands without proper consultation. In lateral leadership, the leadership is still there, but the power is decentralized so that the leader does not fully possess it.

One of the valuable advantages of such a model is its openness to creativity through the sharing of ideas. Since team members can freely channel their own ideas for successfully completing the team's tasks, they gain a sense of belonging and an elevated sense of self-esteem. This fosters a culture of collaboration and accomplishment, which is often advantageous for the whole team.

Of course, there are some people who cannot be productive unless they are reporting to a superior. Such individuals rely on someone to put pressure on them and/or command them to accomplish tasks. In cases of lateral leadership, such individuals might become reluctant to volunteer their efforts, even when other team members seem to be motivated. Instead, they'd rather hide behind their team

---

[15] Koçak, R. D. (2019). *Leadership without hierarchy and authorityLateral leadership*. International Journal of Social Inquiry, 12(2) 657-680. https://doi.org/10.37093/ijsi.659023

members' efforts and wait for celebrations of accomplishment. Unfortunately, bringing out these tendencies in some team members is one of the primary disadvantages of horizontal leadership.

## *Powerless Leadership?*

There is a great deal of information based on the notion that there is no leadership without power.[16] However, I hypothesize that leadership can not only exist without power, but that such leadership is more about responsibility and contribution than authority, positions, titles, and command.

But is "leadership without power" truly powerless? No. However, it is an approach to leadership that is genuinely different from that of leadership with power. Indeed, leaders without power can influence their supervisors regardless of whether they have leadership with power or power without leadership. If you refer back to the titles and leadership subchapter in Chapter 1, you'll note we have made this point from the start.

Powerless leaders can be defined by an exemplary and selfless attitude and an obsession with being responsible contributors. They would show you where to go by going ahead of you, rather than merely pointing out how to get there. Such leaders are highly accommodative and people-oriented, and their leadership qualities are evident even without authoritative positions. Some of the

---

[16] Balogun, S., & Ajayi. (2018). *Leadership strength, personality traits and political mishaps in Nigeria: A call for behavioral change*. Nigerian Journal of Social Psychology, 1(1). *https://nigerianjsp.com/index.php/NJSP/article/download/11/12*

essential attributes of leaders without power are empathy, positive emotions, selflessness, and accommodative body language.[17]

Therefore, we can ascertain that the power of individuals with leadership qualities but without positional authority is not separate from their leadership, but instead embedded within it. This means their leadership qualities essentially lie in their power, because these qualities draw people to them, make them heard, earn them respect, and bestow integrity upon them.

## Leadership and Power

Leadership and power in equal measure are the best recipes for an effective leader, providing the leadership they exhibit can be defined as "good." A person equipped with good leadership skills has control and productive influence, while a person with poor leadership skills can be both dangerous and unproductive. This explanation presumes, of course, that the leadership is somehow separate from power, in which case the power is positional. However, rather than treating leadership and power as separate entities, we must acknowledge that there is leadership with power embedded in it. In this case, the power of leadership is the individual's leadership skills, which can encourage compliance from team members without any coercion. In the next section, we'll look at how leadership and power can work together to create a winning environment.

---

[17] Goman, C. K. (2017, May 21). *3 crucial skills for leading without authority*. Forbes. *https://www.forbes.com/sites/carolkinseygoman/2017/05/21/3-crucial-skills-for-leading-without-authority/*

## *The Capacity of Power in Bestowing Successful Leadership*

In the following paragraphs, I will refer mostly to the power embedded in leadership, which I will refer to as "leadership power." We'll discuss this concept in more detail in the next chapter, but for now, I simply want to look at the overall capacity of power to create a winning team.

### Transforming Idle Power to Active Power

Power is of no use when it sits idle. Therefore, the first role of power in making things happen is its transformation from idle to active. This begins with a leader's realization and recognition of its presence. After all, a leader who does not acknowledge that they have power in the first place cannot be expected to use that power at all – let alone effectively. Therefore, successful leadership is kickstarted by a leader's acknowledgment of their winning power, followed by a commitment to make it productive.

It's crucial that power be proven to work for the leader first. These individuals cannot expect their power to allow others to achieve if it has never allowed them to achieve anything themselves. For that reason, a leader should accomplish whatever possible before prompting their team members to believe they can do the same.

### Influencing Productivity

In most workplace scenarios, team members tend to look up to their leader, which gives them a higher standing and better position from which to influence team productivity. In these cases, the power that influences a team's winning culture could rest in the leader's personality, communication skills, encouraging attitude, direction, or guidance. These factors can also help supervisors' productivity and allow them to important decisions correctly.[18]Similarly, a leader's power is effective if they can make their team members see success from their perspective. Only then will the goal cease to be the *leader's* goal and become the *team's* goal.

## Offsetting Reliance on the Title

Job titles are practically useless if the power inherent in the position cannot make others act. Simply being the manager does not make team members take action, nor does it have any ability to instill a winning mentality. It is how you use your power as a manager that takes the team to the next step. Plan, direct, decide, collaborate, consult—stop relying on the title alone. Wake up and make use of that power!

## Empowering Others

Having power is a valuable first step. But as you progress, you must endeavor not to continue heaping more power upon yourself, but to share it with others by empowering them. Indeed, leadership power should be accompanied by influence, so that good leaders feel self-mandated to replicate themselves. Imagine a world with

---

[18] *Bal, V., Campbell, M., Steed, J., & Meddings, K. (2008). The role of power in effective leadership. Center for Creative Leadership.* https://www.ccl.org/wp-content/uploads/2015/04/roleOfPower.pdf

many other leaders like you! While it is not a simple task, it is made easier by power. Simultaneously, leadership power provides a better position from which to delegate tasks, thereby encouraging a team through hands-on experience. Ultimately, a truly empowering leader is comfortable with collaborations, as they allow both parties to learn from one another.

**Parental Role**

Leadership power used appropriately is channeled toward *caring* for others, not *subduing* them. In these cases, the leadership power should be used to create rules and conditions that are conducive for team members producing their best quality work. In effect, power should be used to make team members feel as if they are part of the process and that their input is appreciated.

Leadership power should also be a tool for helping team members develop socially, emotionally, and intellectually in the workplace. It should never be taken as a license to abuse others, nullify their rights, or dismantle their self-confidence. Moreover, when misunderstandings occur, an effective leader opts for assertive conflict settlement rather than a violent, inconsiderate, or unethical application of force. Of course, the parental role inherent in leadership power should not imply that a leader needs to be satisfied with everything their team members do. Rather, it means that their power should be exercised in a way that is firm, not abusive, and accommodative, not inconsiderate. Likewise, it should always be used with a preference for truth over deception and constructive criticism over corrosive condemnation.

## *Is Wealth Part of the Equation?*

It's true that winning is not always measured by the amount of wealth amassed over time - neither is wealth always an endorsement of leadership power. But is wealth still part of the equation? After all, it is true that wealth has some influence on leadership, particularly in how leaders use their power. For instance, in an organizational setup, increased profits might be interpreted as a reflection of well-managed leadership power. In this case, leadership power is assessed by how much it influences the organization's accumulation of wealth. At the same time, some types of leadership power – particularly those derived from offering monetary rewards to team members as a form of encouragement – are dependent on the very concept of wealth.

In the 21st century, wealth can be considered an effective tool for manipulating leaders. A good example can be found in people who attain jobs, positions, and promotions because of the influence of wealthy parents or colleagues. Indeed, whether they have the required skills and knowledge to perform the job properly or not is rarely considered. This acceleration of individuals into positions of prominence is often done in the interest of attaining more control with which to manipulate the "leader's" positional influence. In short: wealth has the potential to make puppets out of leaders. To make matters worse, team productivity is almost always compromised.

Indeed, wealth can dramatically influence the perceptions of team members and colleagues. This is because wealthy people tend to receive more decision-making influence, even when they lack proper knowledge in the subject matter. Moreover, in situations where a group ends up making their decision, some members might still want to see that decision endorsed by a wealthy person. Put simply: people tend to interpret wealth as evidence of increased knowledge or understanding. Regardless of its value, it is seen as a free pass to instant respect.

However, it's also worth noting that wealth can contribute to positive applications of leadership power, such as those related to investing, donating, and providing guidance through leadership seminars. Such actions can help create better leaders with better power management skills and can be easily made possible via access to great wealth.

## The Wrong Winning Attitude

Is there such a thing as a "wrong" winning attitude? After all, is winning not the most important thing, regardless of how it is achieved? As pervasive as that sentiment might be, I hypothesize that there is such a thing as the wrong winning attitude. Moreover, I feel I would not be doing this book justice if I did not attempt to highlight some of the "red flags" all leaders must be aware of, particularly when winning becomes key to their team's existence. This is because winning the wrong way is actually, in a sense, failure.

### *Misuse of Leadership Power*

Leadership power can be misused. This is particularly evident in cases where getting the "crown" becomes the leader's sole aim.

Examples include using connections to achieve team goals when it is clearly unethical to do so. Another example is when team members become so accustomed to winning without expending the necessary effort that they become lazy, scheming winners upon taking up leadership roles. Both of these examples exhibit the wrong sort of winning attitude.

To make matters worse, they both derive from and result in a leader planting the seed of an unhealthy winning culture, which can create a never-ending cycle unless broken. As a rule of thumb when making a decision or performing a task, I suggest you ask yourself, "how would this look on the front page of tomorrow's newspaper?" If you can honestly answer that the headline would be a positive one, you will likely not do anything immoral or unethical.

## *Shortcuts*

A shortcut is an accelerated route to achievement. For instance, both bribery and trickery are common examples of shortcuts. However, they are neither acceptable nor can they ever direct an individual toward real success. Indeed, in one of his most famous quotes, George Washington Carver said that "there is no shortcut to achievement. Life requires thorough preparation—veneer isn't worth anything.[19]" Put simply, Mr. Carver is saying that any achievement attained the wrong way is no an achievement at all.

---

[19] *George Washington Carver quotes.* (n.d.). BrainyQuote. https://www.brainyquote.com/authors/george-washington-carver-quotes

**Figure 3: Bribes promote the wrong winning attitude.**

## *Fear for Challenges*

Individuals who possess a true winning attitude do not spend the entire journey complaining that the ride isn't smooth enough – they embrace and even pursue challenges whenever they are presented. After all, we learn far more from the challenging experiences of life than we do from those that are easy or direct. Moreover, resilience and other traits desired in a winning team can only be derived from encountering and conquering difficulties. After all, how can one claim to have "won" when there was no opposition in the first place?

Face the challenges, experience the state of not knowing what to do, try an idea to solve the problem, and let it fail.

Afterward, try another solution and then another - until the situation is resolved. This is what cultivates a winning culture and which you can't glean from philosophical lessons alone.

# Chapter 3: Forms of Leadership Power

Leadership power occurs in many different forms. These are, in most cases, are defined according to the sources of power[20], the position of power, and whether the power is personal or corporate. However, no matter how it is classified, the leadership power of all leaders is essentially the same.

## Classification of Leadership Power

Knowing the different leadership types can provide leaders with an awareness of the types of power that foster a winning culture. This allows them to act accordingly in different leadership scenarios. For the purposes of this book, I will divide leadership into two major groups: internal and external.

### *Internal Leadership Power*

Internal leadership power can be defined as a type of power that emanates from within the individual. This makes it far more personal in nature. Internal leadership power is also largely based on the leader's individual attributes, some of which are in-born and some of which are acquired with time. Of course, leadership power

---

[20] Konter, E. (2012). *Leadership power perceptions of soccer coaches, soccer players according to their education. Journal of Human Kinetics, 34(1), 139–146.* https://doi.org/10.2478/v10078-012-0073-x

can be acquired through academic, professional, or personal life experiences, or, in the words of Maurice Flanagan, "some are born leaders, some achieve leadership, and some have leadership thrust upon them. Which of these are you, or would you rather not bother?[21]" If you do bother, let's explore the types of leadership power together.

**Charismatic Power**

While it originally referred to "divine power,[22]" charismatic power reflects an especially unique attribute of persuasiveness in a leader, which can make them immensely popular among their followers. Indeed, the personality of a charismatic leader often gives them the ability to make team members hear and trust them at will. Such individuals are dominant, confident, and have strong opinions. They articulate their goals and vision through passionate speeches, all the while exuding confidence and communicating high expectations. There is far less room for coercion when it comes to this type of leadership. This makes charismatic power a tool of remarkable value when properly used. It is also a critical factor of good leadership, as it increases a leader's chances of having a positive impact and instilling a winning attitude in their followers.

That said, charismatic leadership power is not always linked to good leadership. Indeed, leaders with charismatic power can easily

---

[21] Flanagan, M. (n.d.). *Maurice Flanagan quote*. A-Z Quotes. https://www.azquotes.com/quote/766103

[22] Lindholm, C. (2018). Charisma. *The International Encyclopedia of Anthropology*, 1–3. https://doi.org/10.1002/9781118924396.wbiea1286

manipulate their followers to accept and even take part in unacceptable, unproductive, and harmful behavior. The problem arises from the fact that all charismatic leaders don't automatically possess essential leadership skills such as empathy, active listening, and assertive conflict resolution. This means it is relatively easy to form an autocracy out of charismatic leadership, and hence, also easy for a charismatic leader to misuse their power. In a study ( Collins 2001) of Fortune 1000 companies over a 3o year period, only 11 firms fit the profile of underperforming for the first 15 years and then overperforming for the next 15 years. In all 11 cases, the performance improved because of a new CEO, none of whom were charismatic. If this proves one thing, it is that charisma is not a prerequisite for a leader's success.

**Moral Power**

A leader can influence others through their perception and regard for proper and improper behavior, as well as their willingness to establish good conduct. Such influence is referred to as "moral power," which is also directly linked to the leader's personality. Moral power can encourage loyal subordination in followers who expect that the leader's moral conduct can be used to better themselves or their team. At the same time, a leader who fakes their moral behavior can have the opposite effect by giving the team the wrong impression of their leader. Of course, it is unlikely that any leader with an immoral personality would attempt to uphold proper conduct.

## Engaging Power

Engaging power is an essential asset for leaders who want to create a culture of purpose among their team members. It is characterized by the ability to instill a sense of drive and persistence in one's followers, but without resorting to coercion. Instead, team members are made aware of what needs to be done and then adequately motivated to do it.

Most engaging leaders have grown through the ranks before becoming leaders and are well aware of the productive requirements and conditions related to various tasks. A study by Oehler[23] highlighted the most important characteristics of an engaging leader: people-oriented beliefs and engaging conduct. Ultimately, an engaging leader believes in connecting with their team members and making their working conditions as encouraging and productive as possible. They know that the overarching goal is to accomplish what is necessary as a team.

## *External Power*

External power is, by far, the most common category of leadership power. This is power gained by being in a position where power is available and able to be exercised. In cases where it is not directly linked to a position, external power can result from a leader having

---

[23] *Oehler, K., Stomski, L., & Kustra-Olszewska, M. (2014, November 7). What makes someone an engaging leader. Harvard Business Review.*
*https://hbr.org/2014/11/what-makes-someone-an-engaging-leader*

acquired something that others in the same position as themselves do not possess.

## Legitimate Power

Legitimate power is the control that is vested upon a leader by virtue of them holding a particular job position or title. For this reason, it is also commonly referred to as "positional power." In its most basic form, it gives a leader positional influence exemplified by the right to plan, give instructions, endorse decisions, and supervise. Legitimate power can yield incredible results when coupled with good leadership skills, as it provides a leader with an even better position from which to exert their influence. However, without remarkable leadership qualities, legitimate power can evolve into power without influence. After all, power *controls*, while leadership *influences*. It's also important to remember that legitimate power must be exercised within the limits of the leader's position so as to avoid tapping into another leader's positional territory.

For this reason, a supervisor in one part of an organization is not necessarily a supervisor in another.

## Information Power

When an individual owns information that others need, they are automatically entitled to information power. Of course, the information that results in that power can be corporate, general, or personal – all that matters is that it has the ability to empower others in some way. Corporate information is defined as business and administrative data, such as employee, financial, and customer service information.[24] The relevance of informant power has grown exponentially in the 21st century, thanks to two primary factors. The first is that information has become an indispensable tool for decision-making, planning, procedural activities, and evaluations - all of which are drivers of success. The second factor is that the widespread availability of information means some people may not have access to the right information. Therefore, in this case, the one who possesses information others need is in control.

## Expertise Power

Possessing special abilities and proficiency that other members of the team do not is called Expert Power. One can possess it at specific times or permanently, and it can be gained through either direct experience or via one's academic and professional qualifications. For instance, an expert in using Microsoft PowerPoint presentations will be able to control all proceedings related to executive presentations. Moreover, other colleagues and supervisors will respect the expert's decisions and recommendations because other team members lack that special ability.

With expert leadership power, a team can be driven to excellence thanks to increased certainty of what they are supposed to do and the proficiency with which it is done. Simultaneously, a leader who lacks expertise in a certain area can leverage individual team members' expertise for the greater good.

---

[24] *Definition & meaning corporate information. (n.d.). Dictionary.University.*
*https://dictionary.university/*

In many ways, this is the very essence of teamwork– complementing one another in the process of attaining team goals.

## Coercive Power

Coercive power is the force or control embedded in a leader's positional ability to correct team members through punishment. Under this type of power, team members often do what is expected of them solely because they fear being punished for failure. These punishments can range from verbal reprimands and smaller bonuses all the way up to demotions, suspensions, and even dismissals. Coercive power is of paramount importance in many organizations because it helps order and discipline, keeps employees engaged, protects the inferior and vulnerable, and represses any form of abuse. So while it may have a negative connotation, coercive power is actually highly effective at maximizing team member engagement and focus while increasing their rate of accomplishment.

## Reference Power

Reference power is broadly associated with lateral leadership and is commonly referred to as "reverence power." It is unique because it attracts followers through admiration and respect, sometimes to the extent that followers want to identify themselves with the leader. Indeed, those leaders who exhibit reference power all have one thing in common: strong interpersonal attributes. This means that they can easily interconnect with their team members and possess great acumen when it comes to communication - both things that help them further resonate with their followers.

Additionally, a leader with reference power often has a trackable good record and a reputation for good behavior and fairness.[25] That said, evolving into a leader clothed with reference power does not come on a silver platter - it is a product of hard work and careful investment. Leaders with reference power attain the best possible results by inspiring a winning culture among their team members, often through their own exemplary attitude.

## Connection Power

Connection power is an ability to influence derived from a close association to another influential person. Inter-dependency, therefore, is crucial to this form of power and its effectiveness. And although many people would prefer to call it "networking power," which might seem more appropriate, I prefer to refer to connection power more as a form of "borrowed power." Of course, creating meaningful connections is paramount for any leader looking to build a winning team. According to Michele Jennae, "Networking is not just about connecting people. It's about connecting people with people, people with ideas, and people with opportunities."[26]

The "borrowed power" in connection power works when a leader develops a skill to identify beneficial associations and then establishes an affinity with those individuals. Afterward, they

---

[25] Sowards, M. (2019, October 4). *Council post: How do you build "referent power" leaders in your business?* Forbes.
https://www.forbes.com/sites/forbestechcouncil/2019/10/04/how-do-you-build-referent-power-leaders-in-your-business/

[26] Forsey, C. (2019). *18 quotes about networking that'll help you connect with people.* Hubspot.Com. https://blog.hubspot.com/marketing/networking-quotes

maintain the relationship by creating a unique "fingerprint" that makes them memorable to the people with whom they connect. Once in place, these connections can be leveraged to allow the leader access to power that is not actually theirs. It's also worth noting that borrowed power works less when only the borrower knows the power lender. Indeed, it is far more effective when the power lender knows the *borrower* instead. Leaders who have connection power can accomplish many tasks with greater ease than those without such power. The more associations they can establish, the greater their network capital, and the more the connection power they will possess.

## Reward Power

The influence in reward power is directly linked to the leader's use of rewards to show appreciation to team members. In these cases, the ultimate goal is to encourage their subordinates through positive reinforcement. Rewards can either be personal (if given to an individual within a team) or corporate (if offered to a whole team at once). They can also come in the form of tangible/material or intangible/non-material resources. Either way, reward power is an excellent way to inspire a team or its individual members and can lead to a significant increase in team accomplishment.

That said, reward power can also be counterproductive, particularly if those who do not receive the rewards feel that the receiver's selection was not fair for any reason. This can result in team spirit being thrown off balance, which might lead to divisions within the team going forward. At the same time, a leader can cultivate a wrong winning attitude in their team by introducing improper or unethical ways of getting rewards. Even worse, reward power might shift a team's priorities so that receiving the reward itself becomes the primary goal.

**Material Rewards**

Physical rewards are tangible resources. Perhaps the most common is a salary, which is the standard reward offered as compensation for employees' services. However, team members can be given more rewards, apart from their salaries. Such rewards can be used to motivate individuals further and create a competitive environment aimed at enhancing productivity. These are the rewards that seek to separate the best performers from the rest of the team. Examples of such tangible resources are money, gift cards, certificates, trophies, and vacation days.

**Non-material Rewards**

Though less costly than tangible resources, intangible rewards are also quite effective at motivating team members. Intangible rewards are non-material compensations such as praise, verbal recognition, positive feedback, and on-the-job training.[27] They are sometimes given alongside material rewards.

---

[27] Coleman, E. (2017, October 24). *Intangible benefits that boost employee retention*. Benefits Bridge. https://benefitsbridge.unitedconcordia.com/intangible-benefits-that-boost-employee-retention/

## Political Power

Political power is derived from the support offered by an individual or group of individuals endorsing a person or team's ability to govern a set of resources. This type of power is gained through the ability to communicate persuasively and often involves a wide array of tactics. Generally, political power is characterized by promises of betterment, which a prospective leader offers in return for being chosen through majority selection. Of course, some leaders with political power are merely interested in the benefits offered by their positions. In these cases, their attractive promises only serve as keys to unlock the positions and are not intended to become a reality.

## Founder Power

Founder power is the influence wielded by a leader who is directly associated with the commencement of an organization, either through coming up with the idea or through the act of physically setting it up. This type of power is sometimes influenced by other positional power types within the organization, meaning that a leader can often also use reward, coercive, referent, information, and moral along with founder power.

# Factors Which Determine Leadership Power

By understanding the types of leadership power in play, you might realize that some sound more appealing to you than others. At the same time, some clearly have more pros, where others have more cons, and some will not apply to the dynamics you've currently established for your team. This implies that there are many factors determining what sort of leadership power you should employ. However, failing to identify the right type of power to use may disrupt your team in innumerable ways – even wiping away an existing winning culture.

## *Economic Factors*

Reward power, which is dependent on tangible rewards such as money and other monetarized items, will not be a feasible option when your organization is undergoing a financial crisis. Likewise, when the organization is not lucrative enough to employ individuals with the right expertise for a given task, certain types of expert power may not be exercised. But while economic factors impact some types of power, connection, coercive, and legitimate power are typically not changed.

## *Positions*

Positional leadership powers such as legitimate power, coercive power, reward power, and founder power can only be exercised by a leader who occupies a relevant position. Likewise, connection power may also be classified under positional power if it is established based on positional factors. In cases of demotion, where the position is removed from a leader, the power will be removed as well. That said, moral and charismatic powers are usually not affected by the presence or loss of positions, as they are exclusively personality-based.

## *The Digital Divide*

The digital divide refers to the gap separating those with access to digital devices and the associated technology and those without.[28] In terms of information, the digital divide describes the gap between those who use technological devices such as computers and tablets to access information from the internet and those who cannot access that information on the basis that they do not have the relevant devices.[29]

Of course, individuals on the positive side of the digital divide will possess more information power than their colleagues who happen to be on the other side. In this case, the digital divide, or technology gap, determines who has the information power. However, the digital divide can also affect connection power because those with access to digital devices and the internet can create and maintain more, and possibly better, connections. For a technologically savvy person, just a few clicks provide the information they need and can connect them to relevant people, something that is far more costly for a person without the privilege to do.

---

[28] van Dijk, J. A. G. M. (2006). Digital divide research, achievements and shortcomings. *Poetics, 34*(4–5), 221–235. https://doi.org/10.1016/j.poetic.2006.05.004

[29] Fuchs, C., & Horak, E. (2008). Africa and the digital divide. *Telematics and Informatics, 25*(2), 99–116. https://doi.org/10.1016/j.tele.2006.06.004

## *Birds of a Feather*

Your associations eventually become part of, it not all of who you are. Moreover, the people with whom you spend valuable time are destined to contribute to the type of leader you become, and hence the type of leadership power you exhibit. This is because thoughts, beliefs, hopes, and behaviors are often influenced by one's close associations. After all, birds of a feather flock together.

## *Parenting and Upbringing*

The term parenting is used to describe a parent or caregiver's journey. This journey encompasses all their direct and indirect actions in giving care and protection to a child as well as their

Figure 4: Parenting and upbringing affect leadership power.

influence on his or her physical, intellectual, social, and emotional development.

Upbringing, on the other hand, is parenting described from the child's point of view. It reflects the effects and perceptions of a caregiver's parenting technique in the eyes of the child. All over the world, parenting and upbringing cultivate morals, personalities, perceptions, and beliefs – things that will ultimately contribute to the leadership and leadership power an individual adopts.

For instance, a leader whose upbringing emphasized punishment to instill good behavior will likely subscribe to one of two types of leadership power. The first is coercive power (if they saw value in the parenting method) or reward power (if they grew to eventually dislike that style of parenting).

## *Life's Lessons*

By virtue of their ability to mold personalities and goals, life's hardships play a pivotal role in determining the type of power a leader will use. Indeed, a single life scenario can create different personalities in individuals due to factors ranging from perception and background to emotions and intellect. For example, a problematic situation can create an empathetic personality in one individual while encouraging insensitivity in another. And on account of each leader having different personalities, they will each exhibit different leadership approaches and exercise different types of leadership power.

## *Team members*

Team members are also an important factor in determining which power a leader should use. For instance, a team member who always comes late and sneaks out during work hours automatically calls for the use of coercive power. At the same time, however, the team members' individual perceptions of their leader also define which leadership power will affect them. For example, if the team members admire their leader's good morals, then moral power will work best to encourage them

## Winning Power

So, which types of leadership power will inspire your team and help you cultivate a winning culture? Due to a wide array of factors affecting leadership power, it is virtually impossible to give an honest answer. However, if you make a concerted effort to better yourself and your team members, you can quickly gain an idea of what works best for your leadership situation. After all, it is your team members' perceptions toward your leadership power that will help grow that winning attitude, or cause it to die on the vine.

# Chapter 4: Leadership Power and Personalities

Personalities and leadership power equally contribute to the sort of leaders people become. They also directly affect each other in ways that have both positive and negative effects. For instance, leadership power can drastically affect personalities, while various personality factors can significantly impact the type of leadership power a person employs. In this chapter, I will focus on how different personalities affect leadership power, the factors that define those personalities, and the various types of personalities we already know to exist. Remember this as we go forward: a well-informed understanding of human personality will also elevate your ability to derive complementary leadership power from different individuals.

## Factors Which Dictate Types of Personalities

The broad definition of who we are, in terms of how we think, perceive, feel, act, or react, is called our personality. From a psychological perspective, five widely accepted traits determine what types of personality a person will exhibit.

These are extraversion, openness, conscientiousness, agreeableness, and neuroticism.[30]

## *Conscientiousness*

Conscientiousness is largely associated with diligence, dedication, attentiveness, laboriousness, and carefulness. Conscientious people are good planners, well organized, focused, and rarely allow their direction to be affected by the "prevailing winds." These characteristics imbue conscientious people with a reliable character and the determination to accomplish their goals. By contrast, less conscientious individuals are freewheeling, disorganized, and – ultimately – less reliable.

## *Openness*

Openness can refer to many things, but in this case, it describes a person's readiness to explore new things and appreciate the diversity of life experiences in others. Individuals who lack significant openness tend to be more comfortable with permanent, unchanging situations. They also prefer to stick to "normal" routines and acquired habits.

Those who possess high levels of openness are far more outgoing and stress-free. They are also more likely to embrace a life of uncertainty.

---

[30] Pappas, S. (2017, September 8). *Personality traits & personality types: What is personality?* Live Science. https://www.livescience.com/41313-personality-traits.html

## *Agreeableness*

Agreeableness measures the degree to which an individual is willing to accommodate others and be cooperative. While this is an appreciated trait, it is most often used to identify disagreeable people, who are largely considered mean, uncooperative, and possessing a "no-nonsense" attitude. A key component in agreeableness (or the lack thereof) is the ease with which an individual trusts others. In this case, you must think of trust as an equation: Trust = credibility + reliability + intimacy ÷ by self-orientation (The trusted Advisor, Maister et al.). Disagreeable people are more reluctant to offer their trust to others than those who are agreeable. Stephanie Pappas (2017) also suggests that envy is intrinsically linked to disagreeable behavior because envious people are less comfortable with other people's accomplishments.

## *Extraversion and Introversion*

Most of us know that most people can be divided up into categories of extroverts and introverts. But what does this really mean? From a technical perspective, extraversion expresses the extent to which a person communicates with the environment outside themselves, including – but not limited to – other people. Introversion, on the other hand, describes the extent to which a person works from within. We might say that extraversion is *inter*personal, while introversion is *intra*personal. Most of us will tend to switch between these two worlds during our lives – sometimes from situation to situation. But whether one can truly be labeled an extravert or introvert depends on where they spend most of their time - the external or internal world.

Generally, extroverts are more at home in the presence of large crowds. They are louder and more sociable, and they often find it relatively easy to speak their minds. Introverts, on the other hand, have moments of lone ranging, especially when they are under stress. This doesn't necessarily mean introverts cannot talk or are shy, simply that they are more secretive.[31]

## *Neuroticism*

Neuroticism defines a state in which an individual consistently experiences negative emotions such as worry, sadness, uncertainty, and vulnerability.[32] Neurotic people are emotionally unstable and frequently experience mood swings and depression, even over things they would otherwise consider positive. By contrast, non-neurotic individuals are emotionally stable and tend to control their feelings much better. In leadership roles, stable leaders can effectively manage their team members' and colleagues' emotions while their neurotic counterparts might struggle.

## *Data Collection Techniques*

There are two ways by which humans collect information: via sensing it or via intuition. However, the degree to which we apply either sensing or intuition drastically affects our personalities. For

---

[31] *16 personality types. (2015). Personality Perfect.*
*https://www.personalityperfect.com/16-personality-types/*

[32] *Widiger, T. A. (2009). Neuroticism. In M. R. Leary & R. H. Hoyle (Eds.), Handbook of individual differences in social behavior (p. 129–146). The Guilford Press.*

instance, sensing involves the use of human senses like touch, smell, hearing, taste, or vision to derive information. On the other hand, intuition depends on conceptual possibilities to assemble information, which must be analyzed before making a decision.

There are many situations in which both intuition and sensing can be applied to gather data, especially if the information derived from both methods seems to be in agreement. Yet when an individual is faced with disagreements between the information they gather, they will ultimately rely on the method with which they are more comfortable. To that point, repetitions in the preference of one type of data collection over time will suggest whether a person is sense or intuition dependent. It is also important to note that, to some extent, sensing and intuition also have a connection with whether a person is internally or externally oriented.[33]

## *Data Analysis Techniques*

Thinking and feeling are both indications of how people process the data they gather. Indeed, individuals tend to use both methodologies to attach meaning to that information. However, as with most dichotomies, one method of data analysis will overpower the other based on the individual's preferences. This is particularly evident when thinking and feeling suggest different opinions, decisions, or solutions. Again, in such cases, the technique with

---

[33] *Fretwell, C. E., Lewis, C. C., & Hannay, M. (2013). Myers-Briggs type indicator, A/B personality types, and locus of control: Where do they intersect? American Journal of Management, 13(3).* http://www.na-businesspress.com/AJM/FretwellCE_Web13_3_.pdf

which one is most comfortable tends to become the preference. For instance, thinkers structurally analyze available data and then come up with logical conclusions. They are far less focused on how that data affects people. On the other hand, feelers are more people-oriented and tend to base the bulk of their decisions on their emotions.

## Types of Personalities

Depending on the unique combinations of the above factors they possess, people will adopt their own personalities. For the purposes of this book, I will classify these personalities into the following major categories: director, socializer, thinker, and supporter. This notion is based on the fact that all personalities, including teachers, counselors, masterminds, protectors, performers, champions, as described in Myers and Briggs 16 types of personalities[34] are sub-categories of the four core classes mentioned above. Indeed, many people tend to misunderstand themselves because they cannot distinguish between who they want to be and who they are. For this reason, an honest and informed assessment of the person you are is the foundation of understanding your leadership and leadership power, including how to positively employ the two to develop a culture of winning in your team.

---

[34] Cherry, K. (2020b, September 17). *An Overview of the Myers-Briggs Type Indicator*. Verywell Mind. https://www.verywellmind.com/the-myers-briggs-type-indicator-2795583

## *The Director*

The Director personality describes dreamers who are confident, strong-willed, decisive, and oriented toward achieving goals. "Directors" are also risk-takers - a feature that makes them better candidates for prominent positions in organizations. They tend to approach situations and tasks systematically, and they hold efficiency in the highest regard. At the same time, their characteristics enable them to remain calm and focused, even under stress.

That said, director personalities can also be bossy, mean, and manipulative. Luckily, these traits can be controlled if the individual applies their exemplary leadership and intellectual skills to the task of countering the negative effects of their personality. That said, when a director is under another's leadership, they may find it difficult to cope, as their traits do not often make them great followers.

## *The Socializer*

Compared to other personalities, the "socializer" has a commendable relationship orientation. These individuals can initiate relationships with any other personality quickly and easily because they are so dominantly external. Such a personality encourages socializers to care about what others think, particularly what they think of them. Enthusiasm, creativity, and outgoing nature are the defining characteristics of a socializer, which enhances their ability to thrive in unstable environments and conditions.

In leadership positions, socializers are usually more attentive to their team members' well-being, safety, and satisfaction than other personality types. They are also less bossy and more likely to employ lateral leadership as their mode of operation. However, if not checked, socializers can be less productive when it comes to accomplishing tasks mainly because they may spend too much time talking and creating relationships. This quality can be found in both leaders and their team members, but it is far more detrimental to the team's success when it is evident in the leader.

## *The Thinker*

The thinker personality thrives in the *details*. This is because thinkers are largely driven by curiosity, introversion, and instinct-dependence. Due to their superior mental agility, they are often attracted to tasks that are intellectually challenging or that increase their overall knowledge.

Figure 5: Thinkers prefer intellectually challenging tasks.

As leaders, thinkers may prefer doing things on their own and avoid delegating tasks. This is particularly true if they do not trust their team members to employ the same attention to detail as they would. Alternatively, a leader with this personality may be too skeptical and interrogative to their team members, which can make them appear meddlesome. On the other hand, when thinkers are merely members of a team, they may lose faith in their leader at times, particularly if the leader is less detail-oriented than they'd prefer.

## *The Supporter*

"Supporter" personalities are introverted, calm, humble, understanding, and cautious. They are also task, feeling, and people-oriented, which makes for a unique combination of traits. Indeed, it is rare to find "supporter" personalities in their angry or excited forms, as they tend to be quite reserved when it comes to expressing their emotions. Leaders who have the "supporter" personality are more empathetic than other personality types and display an intense valuation of human relationships.

Although they are highly task-oriented, supports are most satisfied when tasks are completed with respect and dignity. When they are members of the team, supports tend to be hardworking and focused mainly on completing tasks. The primary reasons for this are that their personality is naturally task-oriented and that they want to maintain a good relationship with their leaders and colleagues. Of course, as they are not particularly expressive, they will tend to do what is expected of them whether they are satisfied or not.

## How Personalities Affect Leadership Power

The personalities that most affect leadership power are those of the leaders themselves, as well those of their colleagues, supervisors, and team members. However, all these personalities can, directly and indirectly, affect a leader and their team's ability to complete tasks successfully. In fact, it cannot be overstated just how much different personalities can manipulate perceptions and affect decision-making. This is why understanding colleagues and supervisors' personalities put you in a better position to know what they value, which ultimately allows you to approach them effectively.

### *Effects on Communication Styles*

Different personalities will have differing effects on communication styles, which are essential to demonstrating leadership power. Of course, in affecting communication, these different personalities will also affect how leadership power is wielded. It is also important to note that while a leader's communication style has a more significant impact on a team's ability to accomplish tasks, the communication styles of team members will also contribute to the team's success.

For our purposes here, we can elucidate five distinct styles of communication.

### Manipulative Style

Some communications have underlying intentions that are unknown to the person on the receiving end. However, the reason for the dishonest and calculative communication will vary on a case by case basis. For example, it could be that the receiver would not consent, adhere, or support what is being communicated if they knew the intentions behind it. This type of communication is inherently manipulative, and is often employed by leaders who want to achieve their own selfish goals by connivingly influencing and controlling others.

Whether by leaders or team members, manipulative communication styles do not encourage openness or trust in a team. They might even directly infringe on the rights of others, which is entirely unethical. Moreover, trust among team members will often deplete when evidence of this manipulation is discovered. Therefore, if a leader uses a manipulative communication style, they risk both the misinterpretation and disregard of their future messages once team members learn to recognize the manipulation.

## Aggressive Style

Aggressive communication can relate to verbal, non-verbal, and physically abusive interaction, which violates the rights of the abused person by its very definition. Verbally abusive communication includes any threats that are made or implied through spoken language. Non-verbally-abusive commun-ication refers to threatening gestures that seem to infer menace without explicitly stating it. On the other hand, physically abusive communication is quite obvious, and includes actions as bold as physical assault.

In addition to employing force, aggressive communicators will instill fear and pain in others to get what they want. These individuals are typified by domineering, arrogant, patronizing, and opportunist traits that they then attach to their aggressive communication styles. Aggressive communicators are considered the worst when it comes to fostering beneficial human relationships. They often find it quite difficult to say things like, "may you please," when requesting a favor. Instead, they rely on phrases like "you must," which can ignore the other person's rights. To make matters worse, this type of communication rarely yields positive results, especially in workplace settings. Instead, it only serves to sow resentment, which is not a desired ingredient when creating a winning culture.

## Passive-Aggressive Style

Passive-aggressive communicators, unlike their aggressive colleagues, do not use physical force. Instead, they rely on quiet demonstrations to either get what they want or merely oppose others' ideas and commands. For example, rather than refusing to complete a given task, a passive-aggressive communicator might deliberately accomplish it slowly or schedule it to a later, more inconvenient date.

People who use this communication style can be identified through their tendency to procrastinate, complain, and make intentional mistakes. They are generally bad-tempered and will couple their complaints with an overall hostile attitude. It's worth noting that passive-aggressive communication styles are more common in team members than leaders. Therefore, it is crucial for leaders to look out for individuals who communicate in this manner so they can interpret their message and forge a positive way forward.

## Passive Style

Failure to express one's perceptions, ideas, and emotions in a team environment will automatically put one in a position to yield to others. This is the primary characteristic of passive communicators. In most cases, these individuals cannot engage in debate, let alone conflict. Moreover, passive communicators usually do not maintain eye contact and cannot effectively use gestures to endorse their communication.[35] In fact, they are frequently misunderstood, as their failure to express themselves is often interpreted as a lack of ideas or a consent to the ideas of others.

A passive style of communication is not appropriate for a leader who aspires to lead to win. That said, it can be quite common in team members, so leaders should be on high alert for individuals who display passive characteristics. This is because many passive communicators actually have brilliant ideas that can greatly contribute to the team's success – they merely fail to express them. But a good leader will find ways to penetrate their defenses and encourage them to speak out, which could be as simple as asking them direct questions. This can result in valuable contributions that might otherwise have been lost. Moreover, if this is done regularly, passive communicators can learn to adopt more direct commun-ication styles.

---

[35] Smith, D. I. H., & Larry, M. K. (2015). Gesticulation and effective communication. *International Journal of Linguistics and Communication, 3(1)*. https://doi.org/10.15640/ijlc.v3n1a1

## Assertive Style

Much research has suggested that assertive communication is the most effective of all communication types.[36] Assertive communicators often confidently express themselves in a manner that upholds both their human dignity and the dignity of others by giving the latter an equal platform to express themselves.

In assertive communication, every member in the commun-ication circle is entitled to their thoughts and feelings, and they all have the right to express them without being intimidated or intimidating others. This does not necessarily mean an agreement in discussed issues – just that different views can be placed on the table. The assertive communication method has also been reported to be extremely effective for conflict resolution[37]

Assertive communication is recommended for use by both leaders and team members because it fosters mutual respect and upholds the dignity of all. Therefore, it is also recommended that team members strive to adopt personalities that accommodate this type of communication whenever possible.

---

[36] *Gallois, C., Callan, V. J., & PALMER, J.-A. M. (1992). The influence of applicant communication style and interviewer characteristics on hiring decisions. Journal of Applied Social Psychology, 22(13), 1041–1060.* https://doi.org/10.1111/j.1559-1816.1992.tb00941.x

[37] *Vandergoot, S., Sarris, A., Kirby, N., & Ward, H. (2017). Exploring undergraduate students' attitudes towards interprofessional learning, motivation-to-learn, and perceived impact of learning conflict resolution skills. Journal of Interprofessional Care, 32(2), 211–219.* https://doi.org/10.1080/13561820.2017.1383975

## *Effects on The Leader's Behavior*

In addition to affecting a leader's communication style, personality types can also impact the conduct and mannerisms that mark a leader's behavior. These could refer both to what a leader does in public and what they do behind closed doors. For instance, a leader with a socializer personality may choose to form relationships and talk just for the sake of discussion. Alternatively, they can create meaningful relationships with others and use their talking abilities to increase productivity.

## *Effects on Associations with Others*

It's important to remember that all supervisors, colleagues, and team members will have unique personalities, and they may be quite different from yours. Therefore, knowing each personality type front to back is pivotal to convincing these people to buy your ideas, particularly if their opinion will define whether or not your team is successful. For example, approaching a director personality with a proposal that fails to clearly identify the goal and procedures may be futile, as such individuals are very goal-oriented. On the other hand, a thinker would be more interested in the details involved and the new knowledge linked to your proposal.

Ultimately, a leader who is aware of their team members' personalities can plan and delegate tasks in a more productive way than one who is unaware (or merely doesn't care) to take those personalities into account. Indeed, some tasks are better suited to team members who have personalities that those tasks appeal to, as this will contribute to self-motivation and help ensure the jobs are done with care and skill. For example, researching a project's background information and setting up possible procedures is better suited to a thinker personality than a socializer. On the other hand, a socializer will easily be able to connect with suppliers of the required raw materials due to their social acumen.

## *Conflict Resolution Techniques*

There are many factors involved in resolving conflicts, but there's no escaping the impact various personalities will have on the outcome. The most important thing to consider here is the way that individuals deal with attitudes and negative emotions. There are five ways people resolve conflicts, as developed by Kenneth Thomas and Ralph Kilmann, and these depend on the extent to which assertiveness and cooperation are incorporated in conflict resolution.[38] They are as follows:

### Avoidance

No assertiveness or cooperation exists when avoidance becomes the main strategy for resolving a conflict. In this case, the conflict is merely abandoned without any of the parties' concerns being addressed. In some cases, avoidance will entail the party merely deciding not to attend to a conflict at all or postponing addressing the conflict until emotions subside.

---

[38] *Thomas, K., & Kilmann, R. (2008). Thomas-Kilmann conflict mode instrument: Profile and interpretive report. CPP.*
*http://www.lig360.com/assessments/tki/smp248248.pdf*

Of course, total avoidance of conflict is the worst form of conflict resolution, especially for conflicts of a recurring nature.

## Competition

The competition method presents the conflict as a "win or lose" situation. This means that the issue will either be resolved your way or your opponent's way. For this reason, both sides are incentivized to do whatever is in their power to "win" the case. Each party may do so because they feel they are fighting for a just cause or because they want to avoid losing face, but the approach is the same. While this conflict resolution strategy is indeed assertive, it is not *cooperative*, as none of the involved parties are encouraged to consider the opposite party's point of view.

## Compromise

In the compromising strategy, the involved parties relinquish part of their hold on their arguments, resulting in a resolution that is half win and half lose for each side. In meeting at a point in between the two arguments, partial satisfaction is achieved for both parties. This strategy is primarily successful due to the equal use of assertiveness and cooperation techniques.

## Collaboration

Collaboration also involves the use of both assertiveness and cooperation. In this method, a mediator can take advantage of each party's willingness to consider the other side's viewpoint. Through assertive discussion, the two parties can identify the root cause of the conflict, which would – if ignored - only cause more conflict in the future. Compelling them to solve the problem together makes it more likely that the two parties will find a common solution without one of them feeling as if they "lost" the argument.

Figure 6: Assertive discussion and cooperation are the foundation of collaborative conflict resolution.

## Accommodation

Accommodating can be considered unassertive because one party decides to give up their right to express themselves and be heard. That said, it is still cooperative in nature because the unassertive party considers the other person's concerns and makes efforts to address them. In simple words, one party volunteers to lose in order to resolve the conflict.

An example of accommodating is when one obeys another's instruction when one would have preferred not to do so.[39]

## Managing Differences in Personalities

Every leader who aspires to cultivate a winning attitude in their team should strive to learn the art of managing different personalities. After all, every new team will have a multitude of personality traits at play, and an inability to make each one valuable to the team's goal represents a failure on the part of the leader. To be a winning leader, one must be able to derive success from personality differences. In doing so, the art of delegation and involvement should be viewed as a tool for redirecting differences toward a common goal.

Now, imagine if we all had just one personality. Some tasks would probably be left unattended, as they would require the self-drive that comes from a personality – not an intellect – to be accomplished. However, it's also worth noting that personalities can and do change, and that they can often be infectious in nature. For instance, I've seen people who used to have quiet and reserved personalities who, after mingling with loud and outgoing personalities, began to follow suit.

Remember, identifying personalities that are admirable, productive, and valuable to you, and making efforts to attain them, is always a worthwhile investment. Simply understanding the

---

[39] [39] Thomas, K., & Kilmann, R. (2008). Thomas-Kilmann conflict mode instrument: Profile and interpretive report. CPP. http://www.lig360.com/assessments/tki/smp248248.pdf

differences in personalities is an excellent way to manage them. With a better understanding of each person on your team, you'll know how to properly reach out to the members who will be best suited to a particular challenge or job. You will also know how to win an endorsement from your supervisors while avoiding unnecessary conflicts.

In the end, you and your team can win when you have a better understanding of personalities – including your own.

# Chapter 5: Leadership Styles Versus Leadership Power

There is a strong correlation between leadership styles and leadership power. In fact, it is virtually impossible to talk about one of these topics without leaping into the other. This is because the two factors exhibit a strong influence over one another, which has serious implications for burgeoning leaders. Since we have explored leadership power to a satisfactory extent in previous chapters, we can now examine leadership styles in more detail.

## Leadership Styles

A leader's approach to implementing plans and guiding, motivating, and managing people[40] is called a leadership style. However, there is no "one-size-fits-all" style for all leaders in all scenarios. Instead, leaders often switch between styles depending on the situation at hand, their team members' characteristics, their preferred results, the complexity of tasks, and the time frames in play. I should also note that all leadership styles are coupled with certain types of underlying leadership power from which those styles derive their influence.

---

[40] Cherry, K. (2020a, August 3). *Leadership styles and frameworks you should know.* Verywell Mind. https://www.verywellmind.com/leadership-styles-2795312

Still, an elevated understanding of leadership styles is critical for every leader – even more so for those who aspire to adopt a winning attitude and mentor their team members to do the same. Through this increased understanding, a leader can gain the ability to decide the best leadership styles to employ in any given scenario. The leader can also be enlightened as to how to use their power by positively embedding it in their leadership styles.

There are two major factors upon which the classification of leadership styles depends. These are "task behavior" and "relationship behavior." These factors explain the extent to which a style is oriented toward tasks and/or relationships, as well as what approaches should be engaged in accomplishing them.

## *Autocratic*

The autocratic leadership style is based primarily on command and control. It is a one-way style of communication that comes from the leader and is directed at team members. Opinions and ideas from the team members are not only unwelcome but are rarely sought after. For this reason, all decisions concerning the team and their goals are made by the leader, who assumes they are in the best position to do so. Generally, leaders who embrace this style of leadership will maintain distance between themselves and their team members, which causes human relationships to be neglected.

Research suggests that the autocratic style does not yield productive results,[41] especially in the 21st century, where information is ubiquitous and people of all backgrounds are becoming increasingly knowledgeable. However, there are some instances in which an autocratic style is the best possible choice. Examples include situations in which vital decisions must be made immediately, when there is no time to consult other team members, and when no one else is as knowledgeable about the subject matter as the leader.

**Situational Suitability**

Autocratic leadership is usually applied in situations where there is little room for mistakes. In such cases, total control can be a beneficial tool. For example, in scenarios where mistakes would result in some form of danger, an autocrat's strict rules would not only be relevant, but necessary. Autocratic leadership is also suitable when quick decisions are needed, providing no time for consulting others.[42]

---

[41] Chukwusa, J. (2018, December). *Autocratic leadership style: Obstacle to success in* https://digitalcommons.unl.edu/cgi/viewcontent.cgi?article=5380&context=libphilprac

[42] Cherry, K. (2010a, September 20). *Autocratic leadership. Verywell Mind.* https://www.verywellmind.com/what-is-autocratic-leadership-2795314

## Examples of Autocratic Leaders

### Leona Helmsley

Leona Helmsley is an example of an autocratic business leader who controlled 23 Helmsley Hotels. In her leadership, she was strict with what she expected from the hotel's employees and would not hesitate to prove her point by reprimanding or dismissing those who would no perform as she demanded.

This type of leadership instilled an over-the-par efficiency in her employees, creating a culture that ensured the clientele of Helmsley Hotels would enjoy nothing but the best. In this way, being insensitive, harsh, and unsympathetic to her team members was the primary device in her toolkit when establishing the success of the Helmsley empire. Hemsley is an example of an autocratic leader who believed that when she asked an employee to jump, the answer should never be "Why?" but "How high?"

### Howell Raines

Widely referred to as "hard-charging," Howell Raines was the Executive Editor of the *New York Times* in the early 2000s. During his time at the newspaper, he reinforced a policy he referred to as "flooding the zone," a practice of focusing all the New York Times' resources on covering the stories that he considered important.

All decisions were centralized around him, and he became increasingly scornful to his employees, including the executive board members. In fact, any decisions made in his absence were automatically nullified once he became available again. Editors restrained themselves from raising their concerns in the newsroom, and those who were courageous enough to do so would not get feedback for them[43].

Still, the *New York Times* won seven Pulitzers Prizes in a single year[44] during Raine's tenure. However, his culture of dividing the journalists under him into "stars" and "also-rans" created tension among *New York Times* employees, leading to reduced enthusiasm. In fact, as time went on, there was a marked decline in the quality and quantity of information that the journalists brought forward, which meant lower quality stories overall.

This example shows that, at times, autocratic leadership may work well, but only up to a point where team members can cope with it. Should the autocrat push past this pint, it can lead to open revolts and poor-quality work. As we can infer from these case studies, autocratic leadership can present some advantages, even though many people associate it only with disadvantages. For instance, if there is a type of leadership style that allows things to get done quickly yet efficiently, it is autocracy. But when exercised to the point where resentment grows among team members, it can seriously suppress team morale. Perhaps worst of all, autocratic leadership does not foster team contribution, which causes leaders to miss out on the beneficial skills and ideas that the team members may possess.

---

[43] *Mnookin, S. (2008, April 29). Scandal of record. Vanity Fair. https://www.vanityfair.com/style/2004/12/nytimes200412*

[44] *Jemimasutanto. (2013, April 24). Howell Raines of New York Times. Small Becomes Giant. https://smallbecomesgiant.wordpress.com/2013/04/24/512/*

## *Authoritative*

Authoritative leaders are confident, efficiency-focused, and prefer to implement direct supervision when monitoring their team members. While working with a team, they will set up their individually created vision, and expectations and demand team members follow them to the letter. However, unlike autocrats, authoritative leaders carefully explain their ideas to team members so that everyone is on the same page.

Authoritarians also go to great lengths to foster professional relationships with and encourage individual team members. So, while team members might not agree with the leader's ideas, they at the very least will understand their perspective. Moreover, they will complete their tasks as required because what is expected of them has been made quite clear.

### Situational Suitability

The authoritative leadership style can come in handy when there are strict targets to accomplish. This is because it helps to nail the focus of individual team members to the task at hand. For instance, situations in which unexpected needs arise, including serious emergencies, require authoritative leadership. The same can be said of scenarios where there is a need to boost productivity before a deadline or correct poor performance within an organization.

## Examples of Authoritative Leaders

### Elon Musk

The entrepreneur who founded SpaceX and Tesla Motors hangs his enterprises' success on his own authoritative leadership. Even for the people he hires personally, Musk's expectations are incredibly high, a trait that he feels contributes to the development of high-quality products. Indeed, his primary focus is always on what must be done, even if it means someone must redo a task to perfect it.

Elon Musk couples his authoritative leadership with his ability to make other people, particularly his team members, see the reasoning behind his ideas. In effect, he makes them believe his vision along with him. This means that even though team members may feel that they are working under pressure, they know why it must be done that way. Elon Musk's leadership style has consistently resulted in the best possible products being produced within given timeframes, ultimately leading to one of the top businesses on the planet.

### Martha Stewart

Martha Stewart is a prime example of a leader who dreamt of success and paved her own road to achieving it. Through her authoritative leadership style, Stewart established a position from which she can oversee her entire empire. She is also well known for being a demanding leader who has high expectations for her employees. At the same time, she was innovative in using various media (television, magazines) to become known in households all over America.

Should you desire to include authoritative leadership in your organization, it is essential to understand the pros and cons of doing so. Of course, authoritarian leaders are very clear about what they expect, so it is usually much easier for team members to complete their tasks as required. They also provide valuable direction and can easily explain every step of their vision.

## *Democratic*

A democratic leadership style can be described as participative because it upholds social equality and allows all team members to participate in decision making. That said, the leader guides the decision-making process, so he or she is not entirely silent. This style is known for being highly productive, making it recommendable for creating a winning culture.[45] This high productivity is primarily attributed to the better ideas that arise from team brainstorming sessions and the morale, team-spirit, and mutual respect nurtured by the leadership style.

Although most team members would prefer a democratic leadership style, the concept of involving all team members in decision-making can slow progress immensely. Moreover, this leadership style does not work well when some team members are unskilled, as it usually gives a platform for sharing knowledge that

---

[45] *Bhatti, N., Maitlo, G. M., Shaikh, N., Hashmi, M. A., & Shaikh, F. M. (2012). The impact of autocratic and democratic leadership style on job satisfaction. International Business Research, 5(2). https://doi.org/10.5539/ibr.v5n2p192*

may not be correct or useful. Ultimately, a democratic leadership style is most effective when there are clear boundaries concerning the team members' roles. When these roles are less defined, the effectiveness of the entire method can be compromised.

## Situational Suitability

A democratic leadership style can come in handy when decisions require input from a variety of different skill sets. That said, it is only feasible when there is enough time to allow for the whole consultation process. If time is too short, the solution will fail, and other leadership styles will need to be deployed instead.

## Examples of Democratic Leaders

### Muhtar Kent

Muhtar Kent is the CEO of Coca Cola, where he also serves as the board chairman. He is well-known across the business world for his preference for participative leadership. In his role, Kent is committed to making use of the diversities present in team members to improve business outcomes. To that point, he is as concerned with the efficiency of the company's production process as he is with the satisfaction of the people involved in doing the job.

In other words, Kent is both task *and* people-oriented. Indeed, one of the things that he did to exhibit his democratic leadership style was to employ a collaborative management tactic in response to slow sales numbers. In his mind, a leader who appreciates the power inherent in collaboration will support the notion of shared ideas and decision-making.

**Jack Dorsey**

As the ultra-successful CEO of Twitter, Jack Dorsey is one of the world's top democratic leaders. In his efforts, Dorsey supports the notion of empowering his team and giving them the responsibility to be accountable for their actions. He does not believe in hiding weaknesses, but suggests his team members open up about them so efforts can be made to correct them, all to the company's success.

Democratic leadership is well applauded for the ways that it benefits the group. Not only does it foster creativity and the combination of ideas from team members, but it encourages free expression and acknowledges the presence of different skills in the team members. Like any other type of leadership, it has its share of disadvantages. However, democratic leadership can dramatically elevate team member morale while also seeding a unique sense of belonging in them.

That said, a decision-making process that requires consulting most, if not all, team members can be tedious and time-consuming. Moreover, the democratic style is best suited to teams of skilled experts who do not find it challenging to participate in the decision-making processes.

## *Pacesetting*

Leaders who utilize a pacesetting style are motivated to set high bars in terms of expectations for themselves and their team members. Such targets require maximum effort to meet, so this style can be quite exhausting for followers. This seems to imply that pacesetting leadership is ineffective for long-term application. Indeed, it is far more relevant for single tasks with limited completion time or that require varied results.

## Situational Suitability

The pacesetting leadership style can be easily applied in the face of strict yet short deadlines. It is also useful when high-quality results are expected in those contracted timeframes. It is particularly effective when the team under the leader is highly-competent, well-trained, and self-motivated.

## Examples of Pacesetting Leaders

### Jack Welch

Jack Welch was the CEO of General Electric (GE) between 1981 and 2001. During his tenure, he demonstrated extremely high performance standards, a trait that had him labeled as one of the successful pacesetters of his time.[46] His operation method was largely based on being an exemplary leader who set deadlines that could only be met by the hardest workers.

At the same time, Welch did not subscribe to the notion of micro-managing, which he despised with a passion. Instead, he was known for informally interacting with employees at all levels so that he could inspire them personally. He is perhaps most famous

---

[46] *Pathak, M. (2019, October 15). Pacesetting leadership style.* humancapitalonline.com. *https://humancapitalonline.com/Leadership/details/499/*

for implementing his so-called "Four E's:" energy, energize, edge, and execute.[47]

Welch is also known for rewarding the top 20% of GE performers and relieving the bottom 10% for not performing as expected. This demonstrates just how focused he was on achievement and the successful execution of tasks. Indeed, under the demanding pacesetting leadership of Jack Welch, GE's company value rose by 4000%.

**Virginia (Ginni) Rometty**

In her position as the President and CEO of IBM, Virginia (Ginni) Rometty believed that there was always room for change. At the same time, she was known for applying lots of pressure to influence it. Her main focus was on discovering new opportunities, innovating whenever possible, and always accomplishing set goals. With her pacesetting leadership acumen, Rometty played a significant role in reinventing IBM so that it could accommodate a superior space in the era of blockchain, quantum technologies, and cybersecurity.[48]

The team under the leadership of a pacesetter is more likely to achieve business goals faster, even when given shorter timeframes.

---

[47] *Money-zine.com. (2019). Pacesetting leadership. Money-Zine.Com.* https://www.money-zine.com/career-development/leadership-skill/pacesetting-leadership/

[48] *Busenbark, M. M. (2020, April 23). 6 Leadership styles and when to use them.* www.childrenshospitals.org. https://www.childrenshospitals.org/leadershipstyles

The other advantage is that the team members' skills and expertise are always properly and fully utilized.

This rules out the chance of an employee feeling they have heaps of potential they are not able to showcase. At the same time, the shorter timeframes for completing ensures that updates are done within shorter periods. This helps to identify any issues without delay and allows team members to address them before the set deadline.

Put simply: issues are never allowed to get out of hand. A pacesetting leader teaches the team members how to prioritize their work and reduces time wastage.[49] However, working under the guidance of a pacesetting leader is often hectic and can increase stress and exhaustion levels.

## *Transactional*

Transactional leaders can be characterized by an unwavering focus on performance. In fact, they typically offer incentives and rewards to show their appreciation for the top-performing team members. Of course, they will also institute disciplinary action for performances they deem unacceptable. Fortunately, before such rewards and punishments are prescribed, transactional leaders provide first-hand mentorship to equip their team members with

---

[49] *Ramamoorthy, A. (2019, July 8). Why pacesetting leadership is not always toxic The Upshot Blog. www.upshotly.com.* [https://www.upshotly.com/blog/why-pacesetting-leadership-is-not-always-toxic](https://www.upshotly.com/blog/why-pacesetting-leadership-is-not-always-toxic)

all the tools and information they need to succeed. This makes such leadership extremely useful for achieving well-defined goals.

## Situational Suitability

Transactional leadership should be used where increasing efficiencies, trimming down costs, and improving productivity are the organization's main priorities[50]

## Examples of Transactional Leaders

### Howard Schultz

Howard Schultz began as a Director of Retail Operations and marketing for the Starbucks Coffee Company, which at the time focused on selling coffee beans rather than coffee drinks. Not long after, Schultz became the brains behind Starbucks coffeehouse's launch, an idea he came up with based on Italian Espresso bars.

However, even with the growth that the idea brought to the table, Starbucks' owners still shunned Schultz's ideas. This is why he later left the company and started his own coffee-drink selling venture, Il Giornale. Later, he bought Starbucks from the owners, combined it with Il Giornale, and started running it as CEO and chairperson. And though he started with only 11 regional shops, Schultz eventually grew the business to boast over 300,000 stores worldwide.

---

[50]. Hughes, K. (2019, March 20). *Leading with transactional leadership.* ProjectManager.com. https://www.projectmanager.com/blog/transactional-leadership

Besides establishing a prescribed way of doing things in-store, Schultz reportedly believes that training employees to handle customers professionally should be a business's primary investment. In fact, it's reported that the company spends more on training its employees than it does on advertising and marketing. True or not, it is this commitment that has established and maintained the company's quality of services.

**Tim Parker**

Tim Parker is a transactional leader who, in 2004, took over the management of a motoring company called AA. Upon taking charge, he quickly realized that the company was dealing with rampant inefficiency, loss of employees, and low productivity. Parker further recognized that the previous management team had been incorrectly focusing on extending the brand while neglecting its core business. In response, he began identifying people who were behind multiple inefficiencies and relieved them of their duties. He then focused on increasing AA's productivity. Within the first few months of his leadership, AA's profits nearly doubled.

Understanding the pros and cons of transactional leadership allows us to paint a clear and unbiased picture of what it is. Essentially, transactional leaders establish rewards for team members who perform well while encouraging the whole organization to follow suit. For that reason, the goals set for team members are typically achievable by everyone and serve as the primary basis for incentivizing the workforce.

Of course, not all people are motivated by rewards and incentives. At the same time, the strict goals and procedures preferred by transactional leaders often discourage creativity. This is worsened by the fact that transactional leaders often experience bottlenecks in their decision-making process. This means that team members must often wait to get feedback from the leader before engaging in the next step of a procedure. Not only does this delay the completion of tasks, but it sometimes makes team members feel micromanaged.

## *Coaching*

Identifying talent in followers and guiding them so that they realize their potential lies at the heart of a coaching leadership style. In effect, coaches do not force ideas on their followers. Instead, they encourage team embers to give new ideas a try, which allows them to discover themselves in the process. From a coaching leader's point of view, everyone has power and potential locked within them. All they need is the right leader to encourage them to develop those talents into beneficial skills.

### Situational Suitability

Coaching leadership is most appropriate in cases where there is no time limit associated with the task. This is primarily because such a leadership style leaves room for possible failure, which can't be allowed in cases of tight deadlines. Most experts recommend a coaching approach for smaller groups that allow for the proper development of interpersonal relationships.

## Examples of Coaching Leaders

### Eddy Merckx

A coaching leader begets a better leader. That is the principle that we learn from the coaching leadership of Eddy Merckx, who won the Tour de France four consecutive times. After his victories, Merckx went on to mentor Lance Armstrong, who became a seven-time winner of the same racing competition.

### Andrew Carnegie

Andrew Carnegie was the owner of Carnegie Steel Company and the man whose mentorship propelled Charles Schwab into a steel industry giant. Schwab began his career as an engineer at Carnegie's mill, where he rose through the ranks and soon became a manager. Under Carnegie's mentorship, he was eventually appointed as the company's president. In his testimonial, Schwab said that Carnegie was enthusiastic, kind, and would not blame workers for trivial mistakes – all traits he incorporated into his leadership to great success.

Coaching leaders create an environment that is extremely conducive to their teams' growth by encouraging collaboration, eagerness to learn, and motivation. Through this leadership technique, coaches can quickly identify team members' weaknesses and help convert them into strengths. Simultaneously, existing strengths, which may be unknown, can be identified and encouraged.

Of course, coaching leadership is often tedious and requires a significant commitment of both patience and time. It also requires dedication on the part of the team member, an ingredient without which mentorship cannot produce the required results. Moreover, to work correctly, there should already be a good working relationship between the leader and their team.

## *Permissive*

Permissive leadership is also known as Laissez-faire leadership. In practice, a leader often gives either complete or guided freedom to their followers, ultimately allowing them to make their own decisions. Such freedom is "guided" when the leader provides the relevant materials for team members to complete their given tasks. It is "complete" when team members work independently and only request guidance when necessary. Detractors describe the permissive leadership style as leadership avoidance or non-leadership.[51]

Although permissive leadership is usually associated with low productivity, there are certain scenarios where it can be extremely effective. This mainly refers to situations where team members are already trustworthy, self-motivated, highly-skilled, and boasting some expertise in the subject matter at hand. Still, even in such cases, constant feedback from the leader may be required to ensure the team members are operating in line with expectations.

---

[51] *Skogstad, A., Einarsen, S., Torsheim, T., Aasland, M. S., & Hetland, H. (2007). The destructiveness of laissez-faire leadership behavior. Journal of Occupational Health Psychology, 12(1), 80–92.* https://doi.org/10.1037/1076-8998.12.1.80

## Situational Suitability

There are times when the permissive leadership style is the best approach for a particular situation. For instance, a team that prefers not to be micromanaged often requires this type of leadership to be successful. This is especially true in cases where the team members are experts at what they do and know what is expected of them, or when the task itself requires minimal interference.

## Examples of Laissez-faire Leaders

### Donna Karan

Donna Karan, one of the world's most well-known Laissez-faire leaders, is the founder and owner of DKNY jeans and apparel. Over the years, she has defined herself as a leader who gives her undivided attention to fashion trends in order to keep her company relevant. When it comes to her subordinates, Karan prefers a "hands-off" style of leadership. In her mind, this gives her managers the opportunity and freedom to run the business and make relevant decisions immediately. From her position, she carefully observes her employees' performance and company profit trends but rarely interferes. Ultimately, Karan believes that employees perform better when given autonomy, which raises their job satisfaction and creativity, ultimately yielding increased productivity.

### Steve Jobs

Some would argue Steve Jobs was not a Laissez-Faire leader. But if you ask them why, they often answer that he was too focused on high standards and too quick to fire any employee who did not meet them. But that fact alone is not a good enough reason. After all, the major characteristic of Laissez-faire leadership is a "hands-off" approach. A leader might come in and find things not up to their expectations, but that does not necessarily mean they are not permissive leaders. And this is precisely the type of leader Steve Jobs was. He would hire highly talented individuals and give them the leeway to be creative and productive for him, but always with his own expectations in mind.

The Laissez-faire style of leadership is typically characterized by cons. However, there are some distinct advantages as well. For instance, people tend to learn more when they have no boundaries establishing what is expected of them. This allows for the improved personal growth of the team members, which can contribute to their sense of empowerment.

Additionally, the freedom given to team members by their permissive leader allows them to explore their ability to be creative and innovative. And how about the quicker decision-making process that comes with such a leadership style? The lengthy approval process for decisions is skipped as the team members decide as they deem fit.[52]

All of that taken into account, the team's role can sometimes be unclear, especially when the leader's permissive style is completely hand-off. In such cases, teams will often try to define these roles on their own. If they fail to do it properly, they risk throwing the

---

[52] *Cherry, K. (2010b, September 20). What is Laissez-faire leadership? Verywell Mind.* https://www.verywellmind.com/what-is-laissez-faire-leadership-2795316

project into jeopardy. After all, clarifying "who needs to do what" is a vital step in contributing to any team's success.

Laissez-faire leadership can make it difficult for newcomers to quickly adapt to the organization's systems, which can be particularly unconducive for groups containing non-self-starters. To make matters worse, some people on the team will overburden others with tasks that were supposed to be handled as a group.

## *Affiliative*

The affiliative leadership style follows a servant or "people come first" approach.[53] It is also the leadership style with the highest regard for people orientation. Generally, affiliate leaders identify and support their team members' emotional differences and needs, thereby nurturing productive connections between various parties. This tends to create a culture of collaboration and unity, which can be integral to success.

Team members under an affiliative leader often find themselves motivated by growing a sense of belonging. They are also less likely to succumb to stress because reassurance is never out of their reach. Moreover, should conflicts arise, the leader will have a much easier time resolving them due to the network of connections between themselves and their team members. In effect, they will already understand how to handle the different personalities in play.

---

[53] *Hougaard, R. (2019, May 5). The power of putting people first. Forbes. https://www.forbes.com/sites/rasmushougaard/2019/03/05/the-power-of-putting-people-first/*

## Situational Suitability

The affiliative leadership style should be applied when team members are under stress and may have lost hope for a solution. For example, if an employee were to lose a loved one, this sort of leadership style would help them recover more quickly. Of course, one should take caution not to use affiliative leadership throughout all of an organization's activities, as this can cause an unanticipated shift in the company's goal and mission.

## Examples of Affiliative Leaders

### Joe Torre

Joe Torre was the manager of the New York Yankees from 2011 to 2020. He is well known for exhibiting affiliative leadership toward his team members, particularly in offering them support during emotional trauma. In one example, a player named Paul O'Neill was told that his father had died not long before a game. In response, Torre used affiliate leadership to encourage O'Neill, empathize with him, and glue his focus on the game that they had to play. Under Torre's leadership, O'Neill found the strength to perform - if only to break into tears just after the game ended.

In another scenario, two of Torre's players were faced with challenges concerning their return contracts. Torre used the spotlight of the team's victory celebration shower both men with praise. As a result, they experienced an increased sense of belonging and a stronger sense of unified purpose with their teammates. This encouraged them to work harder to come back next year. As you can see, Torre had a way of guiding his team members' minds away from their troubles and encouraging them to go on.

**Indra Nooyi**

The (CEO) and chairman of the board at Pepsico, Indra Nooyi, is dedicated to forming relationships with her employees while also pushing them toward fulfilling the company's vision. Not only does Nooyi show interest in the well-being of her team members at work, but she also goes beyond the "company gates" boundary to support them as human beings. This is evidenced by a story in which she took time to write letters to several employee's parents, encouraging them to be proud of their children, who were, in fact, members of her executive team.

The advantages and disadvantages of the affiliative leadership style revolve around the style's main characteristics: people-centeredness and a commitment to positive feedback. Affiliative leadership is great for raising team member morale via constructive feedback, which makes team members feel as if they are cared for and considered. This also allows interpersonal conflicts to be more easily solved, as there will already be a solid foundation of good interpersonal relationships.

Teams led by affiliative leaders are known to have less stress. And, in the event they do experience stress, they recover far faster due to the care and inclusion they get from their teams.

## *Bureaucratic*

Bureaucratic leadership is ideally suited to settings in which each team member has a defined work and responsibility. This allows the leader to closely monitor their team and ensure all members fulfill their responsibilities using the prescribed procedures. That said, this type of leadership does not foster creativity or collaboration. Still, in highly regulated organizational departments such as those found in the finance industry, its effectiveness cannot be overstated.

## Situational Suitability

In cases where consistency is required, a bureaucratic leadership style stands out as the best approach. In most cases, it can be used to effectively coerce team members into following proper procedures.

## Examples of Bureaucratic Leaders

### Steve Easterbrook

If you've ever visited more than one McDonald's, you likely noticed it was hard to distinguish one from another, regardless of their location. This is because that restaurant chain has a particular way of doing things that differentiates them from the competition. This procedural way of governing and operating was created and reinforced by Steve Easterbrook. He is the most recent CEO of the brand, and has made a name for himself by developing highly-standardized procedures and control criteria.

All business people who intend to buy a franchise from McDonald's should be ready to follow predetermined guidelines that govern all the brand's restaurants. After all, it cannot be

Easterbrook's McDonald's if it is different in any way from the ones that already exist, be it in Chicago or Cairo.

**Harold Geneen**

Harold Geneen was the President of International Telephone and Telegraph Corporation (ITT) from 1959 to 1977. Under his leadership, the company established strict, predetermined structures within which it would operate. For instance, the organization was divided into tiered departments. Every employee was required to know their respective positions within those departments, thus ensuring they could have very specific roles assigned to them. Operating within this rigid framework, ITT became worth more than $7 billion during Harold Geneen's tenure.

Due to the strict guidelines established under bureaucratic administration, work and play are not mixed. In other words, relationships and tasks are distinguished, which is intended to push team members toward better results. However, since roles are so clearly defined, creativity can rarely be fostered to any degree. After all, in a bureaucracy, a failure to adhere to rules, regulations, and stipulated procedures will be automatically interpreted as a failure to do one's job. By its very nature, this style suppresses competition, whether that competition is healthy or not. Bureaucratic leadership also makes it difficult to instill any form of predetermined change in a company environment. This results in the employees becoming rigid, as they are primarily used to doing what they have been doing for years.

## *Transformational*

The essential characteristic of a transformational leader is that they inspire and motivate their team members to identify and innovate changes that offer new solutions to old problems in the organization.[54] In such a structure, the leader gives their team members the leeway to take complete ownership of their tasks and be decisive in their choices. In many cases, committed team members who thrive under transformational leadership are more likely to become transformational leaders themselves.

## Situational Suitability

Transformational leadership is most relevant in the fast-paced technology industry, where it is easy to be overtaken by the competition. This leadership style is also common in organizations where the mutual trust between the management and the team member is shaky or absent from rebuilding the connection.[55] Indeed, several case studies show that transformational leadership correlates to increased financial profitability in many businesses. Therefore, it can be said that this leadership style can be of use in any situation where a company's revenue needs a boost.

---

[54] White, S. K. (2018, February 21). *What is transformational leadership? A model for sparking innovation.* CIO. *https://www.cio.com/article/3257184/what-is-transformational-leadership-a-model-for-motivating-innovation.html*

[55] Ahmed, A. (2020, March 21). *Transformational leadership examples in business.* BizFluent. *https://bizfluent.com/13725653/transformational-leadership-examples-in-business*

## Examples of Transformational Leadership

### Oprah Winfrey

Dubbed the "Queen of All Media," Winfrey entered the spotlight through *The Oprah Winfrey Show*, which she hosted from 1986 to 2011. She reached many lives through these years, and her program ended up being the highest-rated talk show of all time. And in addition to being the first African American woman to become a multi-billionaire in North America, Winfrey was the overall richest African American of her time.

She also received recognition from *Time Magazine*, which rated her as one of the world's most influential people for six consecutive years, from 2004 through to 2009. However, it was Forbes that gave a confirmatory report of Winfrey's transformational leadership in October 2010. The article highlighted that Winfrey's leadership was focused on her team and vision, as well as her own values.[56] Through this style of leadership, she was able to accomplish her vision while also maintaining influence over her teams and her brand.

### Jeff Bezos

Jeff Bezos, CEO of Amazon, is one of the most well-recognized transformational leaders in the world. He is particularly known for his task-orientation, innovation, and ability to envision short-and long-term goals to meet the public's needs and wants. His

---

[56] Goudreau, J. (2011, October 27). *How To Lead Like Oprah*. Forbes. https://www.forbes.com/sites/jennagoudreau/2010/10/22/how-to-lead-like-oprah-winfrey-own-rachael-ray-dr-oz-phil/

company, Amazon, began as a simple online shop where clients could order hard copies of various books. The company's transformational moment came when it created the eReader, which presented books in their digital form, for purchase and use. This innovation, along with selling a variety of other products, has since elevated Amazon into a trillion-dollar company.

One straightforward benefit of transformational leadership is that it stimulates change.[57] At the same time, it enhances the unity of purpose in teams, which has the added benefit of trimming turnover rates. Indeed, a high turnover rate costs the company money and resources since it has to search for, employ, and probably train replacements for the employees who leave. But transformational leaders are usually better communicators than their peers, which makes them great at building and sustaining team members' morale.[58]

In general, transformational leaders are driven by an undivided focus on clear and authentic values. This helps them instill the same culture in their employees. And while some team members may feel pressured when they operate under a transformational leader, most will thrive.[59]

---

[57] Charalambous, M. (2019, December 16). *The pros and cons of transformational leadership.* www.startingbusiness.com. *https://www.startingbusiness.com/blog/transformational-pros-cons*

[58] Thompson, J. (2019). *Advantages and disadvantages of transformational leadership.* Chron.Com. *https://smallbusiness.chron.com/advantages-disadvantages-transformational-leadership-20979.html*

Transformational leader's grip is based on their team members' loyalty, which is mainly accomplished by their adopting the leader's vision for success.[60] Regular communication of the goals is a necessity, as is constant feedback on the team's progress toward them.

## Factors Affecting Leadership Styles

Numerous factors influence the type of leadership that a leader can apply. These include internal factors from within individuals or external factors emanating from the environment. In many cases, a single factor can dominate all other factors in determining a leadership style. Alternatively, a combination of factors may be considered when a leader is determining what style to employ. Remember, as I mentioned, one leader can adopt many different leadership styles. However, appropriately determining the right style for a specific set of conditions is dependent on a sound knowledge of all factors affecting leadership styles, as described in this section.

### *The Leader's Personality Traits*

A leader's personality traits are some of the internal factors that affect their choice of a leadership style and will usually determine the leader's main leadership style on a typical day. This is because the leadership style suggested by these personality characteristics

---

[60] *Charalambous, M. (2019, December 16). The pros and cons of transformational leadership. www.startingbusiness.com.*
*https://www.startingbusiness.com/blog/transformational-pros-cons*

come more naturally to the leader. For example, a leader who thrives best under competitive environments will probably adopt the pacesetter leadership style. This will appeal to their tendency to have an "I will teach you how it's done" attitude.

## *Time Frames*

The period during which a team needs to complete a given task is a significant factor whenever a leader is deciding on which leadership style to employ. After all, some leadership styles are time-consuming and can only be used for tasks with longer time frames. But the opposite is also true. Indeed, more interactive and brainstorming-based leadership styles won't be suited for tasks with limited time frames. If they are applied anyway, the team may risk failing to complete the task before the deadline. When time is short, it's best to embrace leadership styles that operate on a "one-way communication" or "command" principle. These include both the autocratic style and the authoritative style. However, keep in mind that the latter can only be employed if the given time frames can accommodate the task's explanation by the leader.

## *Personalities of Team members*

Team member personality traits will significantly impact whether or not they thrive under certain leadership styles. In fact, as different as their personalities are, so too will be their responses to different leadership styles. Usually, team members perform better under leadership styles influenced by personalities similar to their own, or to the sort of personalities they admire. For instance, a thinker personality will perform better under a pacesetter leadership style than a socializer would. Likewise, a democratic leadership style will favor the performance of supportive and socializer personalities.

## How the Leader Was Mentored

A leader is highly likely to adopt the same type of leadership style under which they were mentored. This is especially true if they rose to more significant positions under that direction. However, if the leadership style under which they were mentored did not work well for them, they might choose to adopt it only because that is the style with which they have the most experience. On the contrary, they may opt to try another style due to the resentment they still bear for their mentor's approach.

## Experience and Skills of Team Members

The experience and skills that team members adopt over time are essential in choosing a leadership style. Be their hands-on experience or intellectual skills, they can also determine how team members perform under certain leadership styles and whether or not they will be productive. Indeed, each team members' skills suggest whether they need direct supervision or not, and whether they need more time to complete specific tasks than their peers. Where more skilled and experienced team members will presumably take less time to perform some tasks, their less experienced colleagues are likely to spend considerable time on trial and error. Therefore, leadership styles in which the leader is less engaged, such as Laissez-faire, can still be productive, but only if the team members are more skilled and experienced.

## *Scenarios and Type of Work*

It's important to consider the nature of each situation and the type of work being performed when choosing a leadership style. This helps one select a style that serves the relevant purpose and sends the right messages. For instance, one cannot use a democratic leadership style in a punishment scenario; otherwise, the reprimand may lose its weight. In this case, an autocratic style would be far more appropriate. After all, this is not a time for the subordinate to air their views, but to realize that their behavior is unacceptable, no matter their reasons.

## *The Motivation of the Team Members*

What are your team member's sources of motivation? Is that motivation internal or external? If it is the latter, you must then determine whether the motivation is tangible or intangible. This is because an internally motivated team member will be self-driven and productive under both permissive and pacesetting styles. If external, intangible rewards such as praise and encouragement will be far more effective, meaning coaching and affiliative leadership styles would be most appropriate. When motivation is external and tangible, a transactional approach would be best. After all, they would want to receive some incentives in appreciation for their commendable performance.

## The Mutual Influence Between Leadership Styles and Leadership Power

Although leadership power and styles are separate and independent variables of leadership, they do impact each other. Indeed, an informed realization of the relationship between the two can remind leaders that when they choose to adopt a certain leadership style, they automatically endorse the application of some type of power (and vice versa).

### *External Power and Leadership Styles*

As explained in Chapter 3, external power refers to all forms of leadership power that originate outside the leader's inner being. To that point, there are some distinct correlations between external power and leadership styles. For instance, coercive, legitimate, and reward power—all external forms of power—are associated with the transactional leadership style.[61]

Moreover, these leadership types and styles have something in common: both are based on an exchange taking place between the leader and the team members. For instance, a team member must competently complete a task to receive a salary increase when reward power is at work. Alternatively, they will be punished if their performance does not measure up to expected standards—which is an example of coercive power.

---

[61] *Ojo, A., Ree, M. J., & Carretta, T. R. (2016, April 22). The correlation between leadership style and leader power. Apps.Dtic.Mil.* <u>https://apps.dtic.mil/sti/citations/ADA631959</u>

Both instances are an echo of how the transactional style of leadership operates. Expert and referent leadership power is associated with the transformational leadership style. In this case, the styles and power are based on the foundation that they help the team members exceed expectations. Moreover, in both the transformational leadership style and the expert and referral power, mentoring plays a pivotal role in helping the team member excel.

## *Internal Power and Leadership Styles*

Internal forms of leadership power, such as charismatic and moral power, are strongly associated with the behavioral fingerprint of the leader. At the same time, the personalities of leaders also affect their leadership styles. Therefore, personalities are the common ground for both internal leadership power and leadership styles, and they aid the influence of both on each other. For instance, a leader's good morals can impose moral power on them, which determines their main leadership styles (say, for example, the affiliative style). Alternatively, good morals may influence the leader to prefer the affiliative leadership style, enabling them to exert moral power on their team members.

## *Team Member Power and Leadership Styles*

The team members' perceptions of their leader and his or her leadership power is what I refer to as "team member power." And while leadership power works from top to bottom, team member power works from bottom to top. And while this is not a typical power structure, its impact on leadership styles cannot be ignored. This relationship exists because the perceptions team members have of their leaders tend to affect the team members' personalities. In turn, these personalities will impact the leadership styles employed by their leader, creating a cycle. So, if the team's perceptions of their leader's power cause them to become more assertive and arrogant, the leader may opt to embrace a more forceful leadership style, such as the autocratic style. Of course, team member power does not always result in negative behavior. For instance, if the team members' perceptions are positive, they are likely to cause positive changes in the team member's personalities.

Figure 7: Team member power is based on the perceptions of the followers on their leader.

Another crucial aspect linked to team member power is social power. This is defined as the potential of an individual to influence their colleagues to initiate any form of change.[62] Social power may result in shared perceptions by the team members and, depending

---

[62] *Atwater, L. E., & Yammarino, F. J. (1996). Bases of power in relation to leader behavior: A field investigation. Journal of Business and Psychology, 11, 3–22.* *https://doi.org/10.1007/bf02278251*

on whether the influence posed by social power is positive or negative, productive or detrimental results should be expected. Examples of productive results might include higher self-motivation and improved performance, while examples of detrimental results might include everything from reluctant compliance to outright insubordination.

## Don't Fake It

Clearly, all leaders deeply consider the leadership styles they want to employ, as these have an undeniable influence on their leadership power. By way of long-term effects, the leadership style they choose will be a determining factor in whether or not a winning culture can be cultivated in their team. However, the most important thing to remember is that making the wrong choice of leadership style can ultimately derail your dream of being a successful leader, which is an even worse fate.

Here are a few steps to help you identify the right leadership styles for creating a winning team:

1. Be honest and identify yourself.
2. Acquire an in-depth understanding of all leadership styles before you choose your own.
3. Begin with and continue practicing your preferred leadership style.
4. Develop the ability to switch leadership styles to suit different scenarios.

# Chapter 6: The Hidden Motive

A motive is a need, desire, or emotion that either creates or enhances a person's will to do something. In many ways, a motive provides an answer to the question, "Why am I doing this?" For example, I am drinking water because I am thirsty. Here, drinking is the action being encouraged by the motive of thirst. As in the example above, some motives are apparent, while others can be hidden and known only to the individual performing the action. Unfortunately, hidden motives are often misinterpreted by others, leading to both positive and negative results. In this chapter, I'll provide you with an overview of motives so that we can extrapolate the roles they play in fostering a winning attitude in both leaders and their teams.

## Types of Motives

Psychologists have been studying motives for decades, and have classified them into three major categories: physiological, social, and personal. Indeed, all of the motives that fall under these categories are meant to satisfy specific wants, needs, or emotions. To give you a better understanding of what we mean, we'll discuss each category in detail.

## *Physiological Motives*

Physiological motives are also known as biological or primary motives. The broad goal of all motives that fall into this category is "homeostasis," which is the maintenance of a stable environment inside our bodies. When changes occur inside our bodies that disrupt homeostasis, our body will send us a message, usually in the form of discomfort. This is intended to motivate us to restabilize our bodies. For instance, when we are thirsty, our mouths will feel dry. When we drink water, this sense of dryness can be relieved.

Now, looking over the motives described in this section, it might be difficult to imagine how they apply to leadership power. However, as you'll see, there is more to them than meets the eye. Remember, even the little foxes can spoil the vine.

### Hunger and Thirst Motive

Food and fluids are basic needs for all human beings, leaders and team members included. When these are depleted, we will feel hungry or thirsty. And once we satisfy these needs through eating or drinking, the food and fluids are used up by various biological processes. However, when these needs are not satisfied, both leaders and team members can become unproductive.

### Temperature Regulation Motive

The normal body temperature in humans is 99 degrees Fahrenheit or around 37 degrees Celsius. When our body temperature increases, our body will react by sweating. When the opposite happens, our body will often respond by shivering. Both of these responses indicate that we should take steps to stabilize our body temperature. We might do so by wearing a heavy jacket or sweater to warm us up when we are shivering or removing a layer so we can cool off. Now, think about it, do the temperature conditions in your workplace ensure this motive is properly respected?

## Sleep Motive

Sleep is a fundamental motive for all human beings. Without proper sleep, humans can suffer from drained energy and hampered productivity. At the same time, sleep deprivation can cause confusion, depression, inability to concentrate, and chronic cases that may cause high blood pressure, heart attack, and stroke.[63] The sleep motive requires that one has ample time to sleep, and this applies to both team members and leaders.

## Waste Elimination Motive

In maintaining a stable internal environment, our bodies generate waste to be eliminated. It, therefore, has mechanisms that perform this task. Excess water and other salts can be expelled from the body as urine and sweat, while solid products of digestion are removed as stools. Facilities that properly encourage the fulfillment of this motive are likely to impact team morale and mental preparedness.

---

[63] *Matricciani, L., Bin, Y. S., Lallukka, T., Kronholm, E., Wake, M., Paquet, C., Dumuid, D., & Olds, T. (2018). Rethinking the sleep-health link. Sleep Health, 4(4), 339–348. https://doi.org/10.1016/j.sleh.2018.05.004*

## Pain-Avoidance Motive

Both the conscious and unconscious avoidance of pain is a natural motive. Indeed, we all tend to avoid situations where we might experience pain to some degree. This response is sometimes automatic, such as when we accidentally touch a cooktop, and our body responds by pulling back our hand. Safe workplaces and safe tasks are best for accommodating this motive.

## Sex Motive

This motive is triggered by sex hormones such as testosterone and estrogen. But unlike the other physiological motives, the sex motive is not critical to individual survival, just the survival of the species. Also, unlike hunger and thirst, the sex motive is guided by laws and regulations that form boundaries regarding how this motive can be satisfied without infringing on others' rights. It's important to note that this motive is often misused in team situations. In fact, in some cases, the sex motive becomes the replacement for hard work and exceptional performance when leaders issue rewards.

## *Social Motives*

Social motives, also referred to as secondary motives, are adopted by individuals through their interaction with other people in their social circles. The strengths of these motives vary from individual to individual, as the extent to which people interact and the effects of those interactions are never identical. Moreover, the interactions that trigger social motives are not always direct. Indeed, some individuals choose to distantly observe other people, creating the desire to imitate them.

## Achievement Motive

The desire to reach set goals is called the achievement motive. Such zeal derives from observing high achievers in one's social circles. This creates a motive defined by an "if they did it, I can do it too" attitude. Individuals driven by this motive often set high goals, choose challenging tasks, innovate often, and value all feedback on their performance to improve. Achievement-motivated individuals are commonly successful at employing a pacesetter leadership style and thrive under such leaders as team members. In some cases, the achievement motive is the result of parenting and upbringing that encouraged exceptional performance. This typically includes the provision of relevant educational skills and fostering of good morals, both of which help develop an unwavering focus on goals.

## Power Motive

The power motive is at work when an individual desires to rule, instruct, command, enforce laws, and have subordinates under their command. Power is the main concern of power-motivated people because they see it as their primary weapon for influencing others. Power-motivated people are satisfied when their instructions are followed to the letter and may resort to punishment in instances where they are ignored.

## Affiliation Motive

The affiliation motive is driven by gregariousness, which refers to an individual's propensity to develop, establish, and maintain relationships with members of a certain group. It is often accompanied by a readiness to follow and fulfill all the groups' expectations. At its core, the affiliation motive is driven by a need for safety and security, which come from being part of a group. This motive is common in those who desire a sense of belonging and want to subdue feelings of loneliness and low self-esteem.

## Aggression Motive

The aggression motive describes an individual's readiness to resort to hostility in the face of anger, bitterness, and disappointment. There are three forms of aggression such a person may choose to apply: verbal, physical, and silent. Of course, both the verbal and physical aggressive motives will seem more evident than the silent one. This is because silence is typically employed by passive-aggressive people who are unable or unwilling to verbally or physically air their frustrations. They, therefore, "speak" through silence.

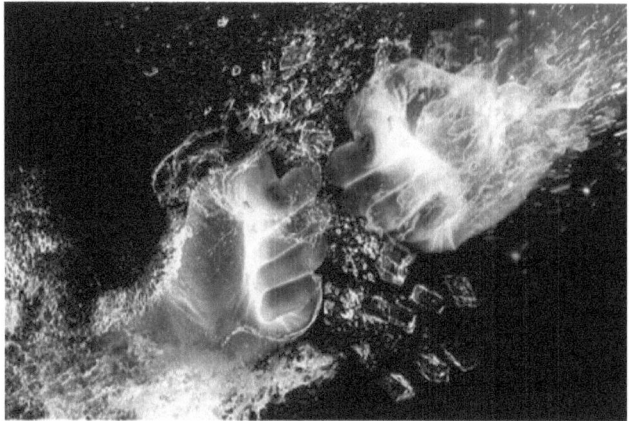

Figure 8: The aggression motive.

## Curiosity Motive

Also known as the exploration or stimulus motive, the curiosity motive involves the desire to search, discover, experience, and know new things. Individuals with this type of motive tend to look at things from new and interesting angles. Indeed, those who exhibit a "thinker" personality are often motivated by curiosity. You'll commonly find these individuals expressing a desire to travel to far off places to see something new.

## Acquisitive Motive

Humans will always desire to acquire things they find attractive, whether they "need" them or not. Therefore, we can say that the acquisition motive is based on the "want" to acquire material things, usually in the form of money and property. Typically, this motive develops due to a person observing those who have a desirable lifestyle that is tied to property acquisition.

## *Personal Motives*

Personal motives are not entirely separate from physiological and social motives. In fact, most personal motives would fit rather well in these categories. However, the primary difference separating personal motives is that they are individualized to a much greater extent.

### Levels of Aspiration

An aspiration is a strong desire to achieve something or live with purpose. Many different factors affect the level of motivation associated with the aspiration motive, which is what mainly defines its individualization. Indeed, even if two individuals' level of motivation were the same, their efforts to fulfill those aspirations would not be. Moreover, the satisfaction felt upon achieving these goals is also dependent on the level of aspiration and consequently guides how lofty the goals may be. For instance, let's assume (in terms of percentage) an individual sets a 50% success target. They are likely to be satisfied even if they reach only 35% success. However, a person with a 95% target could never be satisfied with 35% achievement. Therefore, the higher the aspirations, the higher the performance, and the higher the achievement. When discussing the aspiration motive, it's important to match aspirations with abilities. This will help avoid the frustration that results from an individual setting high goals without the comparable skills to accomplish them.

## Habitual Motive

A habit is a regularly repeated behavior that is done either consciously or subconsciously. Though we tend to think of most habits as "bad," they can be good as well. For instance, if an individual has a habit of regularly exercising, the habitual motive will remind them to exercise again the next day. Such actions as smoking, reading, brushing one's teeth twice a day, meditation, and alcohol consumption are all subject to habitual motives.

## Personality Motive

Attitudes and interests are highly personalized, which is why individuals display so many different personality types. In some cases, a person's personality will be typified by their motivation to indulge in tasks, which another person with an opposite personality would never consider. Of course, those who do things that align with their personalities are more likely to do them better.

## Goals Motive

Goals are themselves a form of encouragement for the people who set them. These goals can be occupational, educational, or sporting, among others, and are often affected by factors such as the person's intellectual capacity, information, parenting, upbringing, and personality. This reminds me of when I was young. We had little access to information back then, so the people we most admired were the teachers we met at school and the doctors we saw at our local hospital. We thought those were the only good jobs a person could have, and so we started dreaming of becoming one or the other. It wasn't until we grew older and became more exposed to the outside world that our goals changed. So, yes, goals can change depending on the multitude of factors that affect them.

## Motives and Leadership Power

Motives drive leadership power. That said, it can be challenging to derive correct interpretations of motives at all times. This is because people rarely say what they mean, and their actions are not always entirely authentic. Therefore, motives can be interpreted from different standpoints. We can also say that the more authentic interpretations of motives are those that remain the same, even when considered from very different perspectives. Above all, this section recommends that leaders and their team members be motivated to create winning attitudes by setting the right motives, particularly those common to the whole team.

### *The Leader's Viewpoint*

From the leader's viewpoint, the motive of leadership power is dependent on the personalities of both themselves and their team members, their leadership style, and the type of leadership power they enjoy. For this book, I am of the mind that all the involved factors, since they are ultimately interrelated, should point toward the main motives of the leader's power.

Allow me to explain.

If a leader has a thinker personality, a pacesetter leadership style, and expert power, that leader also has an achievement motive. If a leader does an honest "motive check," they can get a better idea of their motive orientation. This helps them fill in the gray areas in their actions and allows them to correct those tendencies that might be unproductive. Of course, a leader's personal motives cannot be ignored because they directly reflect on the leader's social motives. Similarly, each leader's habitual, personality, goal, and aspiration level motives should be revised where and when necessary to ensure they align with achievement and can cultivate a winning mentality in their teams.

On that note, there are some motives every leader who aspires to cultivate a winning team should avoid. The aggressive motive is a great example. Another is the sex motive. While the latter motive is - to a certain point - natural, leaders can cause problems when they don't consider how and where they satisfy it. For instance, it should never be satisfied at work or by team members, colleagues, or supervisors. Remember, your team members are watching, and you need to create a foundation of trust if you want to build a winning culture. Should your team members label your behavior negatively, it will impact their perception of you and hurt your ability to influence them.

## *Team Members' Viewpoint*

How do your team members interpret your motives? After all, not all motives are oriented toward a winning attitude, so what they see in you will either carry your vision forward or ultimately destroy it. Some of the primary ways in which they interpret your motives are by analyzing how you communicate to them, organize them, and deal with conflicts. Remember, your actions speak louder than your words, and these actions that we so often call "the little things" really do matter. For instance, do you acknowledge their entitlement to physiological motives as you would your own? If you push them to work day and night, your actions are telling your team members that their sleep motive doesn't matter to you. And should they interpret it in that way, their desire to cooperate with you will be compromised.

Now that you understand motives better, try using this information to mold your behavior and present motives that suit a leader who wants to win. In doing so, the most important thing is to ensure the perceptions of your team members identify you with winning. From there, you can develop and establish good relationships with your team members and make their working conditions comfortable to the best of your ability.

## *Fostering Common Motives*

Creating a team with common motives is not easy. It often entails aligning the physiological, social, and personal motives of every team member with, in this case, the team's achievement. This all begins with encouraging the achievement motive present in each individual, then weaving that into a collective achievement motive. In this section, we'll highlight some tips to help you accomplish that.

### **Present Transparent Goals**

The team should be well-versed in the objectives they need to achieve. If there is any specified priorities or time frames in play, those should also be made quite clear. This gives the team a sense of responsibility, which is integral to cultivating winning attitudes.

## Regular Reports and Feedback

Although a leader should limit micromanaging, constant reporting and feedback procedures help them maintain professional contact with their team members. This allows challenges to be quickly identified and solved while new ideas can be communicated and incorporated. Overall, constructive feedback helps the team members know if they are on the right track and where they need to apply more effort.

## Timely and Fair Compensation

Hunger, thirst, and acquisitive motives encourage people to work hard and keep busy. However, there is no point in performing well in a workplace where leaders take these motives lightly in the form of untimely and unfair salaries. Ultimately, fair and timely compensation can foster common motives for winning in a team.

## Work Environment

A work environment should be as comfortable as possible for team members in order to create and maintain morale. This includes a clean, well-maintained restroom to satisfy the waste elimination motive and equipment that is continually evaluated and serviced to ensure the team is safe and secure. The atmosphere should accommodate the affiliative motive and make it highly unlikely that the pain avoidance motive will be applied. In the end, team members are more dedicated to fulfilling set goals when their welfare is among the leader's priorities.

# Chapter 7: The Influence in Leadership Power

On its own, power is enough to force team members to complete given tasks without considering their willingness and understanding of the procedure. Influence, on the other hand, still accomplishes tasks. However, team members are given a clear understanding of what must be done, as well as how and why. Therefore, influence makes the team members part of the entire process leading up to the completion of the task, something that is widely associated with higher productivity.

Considering that some aspects of leadership influence have been covered in previous chapters, this chapter will touch on those that remain. Specifically, it is aimed at making leaders understand how much influence they have over both their power and the development of a winning culture.

## Influence on Gender Bias

There is an unignorable cry about gender imbalance all over the world, particularly from women. Of course, leaders are best positioned to accommodate all gender affiliations and instill the same mindset in their team members through their influence. This means acknowledging that an individual's gender affiliation is not a reliable variable in assessing their ability or productivity.

Moreover, every leader who aspires to be effective in their influence should be aware of both conscious and unconscious gender bias at all times.

## *Conscious Gender Bias*

Gender bias can sometimes be clear, open, and deliberate. This is called conscious gender bias. There are many ways both leaders and team members exercise conscious gender bias, including:

### Married and Pregnant

Refusing a female's attempt to join your team because they are married, pregnant, or breastfeeding is gender discrimination. This displays a mindset that believes women should stay at home as they are inferior and/or incapable of work. If a leader is particularly unempathetic, they may not realize that such accommodations need to be made to counteract this bias.

### "Female-Based" Gender Bias

There is another type of gender bias that is unique and rarely discussed. It involves women in leadership. Though it is unclear whether this phenomenon is due to a fear of competition, insecurity, or lack of confidence, the result is that some female leaders tend to be more aggressive with female team members than males. This, in turn, causes female team members to be less supportive of the female's leadership. This kind of conflict cannot foster a winning attitude in the team. Luckily, since female leaders understand the aspects of being female much better, they are better positioned to use their leadership power to motivate and elevate other women.

## *Unconscious Gender Bias*

Although efforts are being made in different organizations to fight against gender bias, unconscious bias against women persists. This refers to orientations or opinions based on gender without the intention of doing so.[64] This bias can seriously hamper a woman's progress in her career, assuming she is given a chance to pursue one at all. That said, I believe some men are also affected by unconscious gender bias. Leaders who want to create a winning culture should do their best to erase unconscious gender bias from both themselves and their team members. To give you a better idea of how to accomplish this, let's discuss some ways in which unconscious gender bias can crop up.

### Recruitment Processes

Some recruitment requirements are gender-segregated. For instance, requirements that present masculine recruitment criteria inevitably leave females out, even when they are perfectly capable of delivering. The same applies to feminine-oriented requirements, which segregate males. In most cases, these requirements do not directly stipulate whether a male or female is preferred but will instead use words like "aggressive," "confident," and "goal-

---

[64] *International Labour Organization. (2017). Breaking barriers: Unconscious gender bias in the workplace.* http://www.oit.org/wcmsp5/groups/public/---ed_dialogue/---act_emp/documents/publication/wcms_601276.pdf

oriented," which are mostly oriented toward men. The same applies to promotions defined according to masculine or feminine properties. These narrow the chances of the gender not stipulated in the requirements being fairly considered. Leaders who want to create a winning team should be comfortable with both a diversity of abilities and gender.

### Assignment of Tasks

Unconscious gender discrimination can be reflected in the way tasks are assigned among team members. Sometimes, the leader does not mean to undermine a team member simply because she is female, but they still show concern and protect them. For example, a leader may assign more challenging assignments to males while giving their female team members more comfortable roles. Since a woman who is allowed to complete more difficult tasks is automatically given a chance to rise and be recognized, leaving her out can curb her career growth. Ultimately, assignments distributed based on gender diminish the chances of making productive use of the team's abilities, some of which can only be seen and appreciated through challenging assignments. Remember, in a winning team, no resource should be undermined!

### Unconsciously Attacking Language

Some very specific traits have become associated with males or females over the years. Still, it is extremely unprofessional to define situations, actions, or results according to gender affiliations. Suppose you visit the restroom at work and you find it dirty. You couldn't say something like "new team members are so messy!" in response. After all, it could have been existing team members that made the mess, and you would be inadvertently showcasing a hidden bias. In the end, making use of accommodating and inclusive language is an art worth learning. It lowers the chances of your unconsciously attacking others and reduces distractions that might negatively affect the team.

## Influence on the Vulnerable

One of the things leaders can do to build a winning culture in their team is make an effort to ensure their team members' emotional stability. Emotional instability can be caused by depression, grief, fear, anxiety, and trauma, and all of these may be linked to various levels of vulnerability. Vulnerability is a position of being exposed to physical or emotional harm.[65] Obviously, it would be quite difficult for a team member to be productive when emotionally unstable, which would affect the team's overall productivity.

### Harassment in the Workplace

If any of your team members face abuse at work, be it physical, sexual, or emotional, their ability to concentrate on tasks will be impaired. It is within the duties and power of a leader to immediately resolve workplace harassment issues when they are brought to their attention.

---

[65] *Vulnerable. (n.d.). Merriam-Webster.Com.* [https://www.merriam-webster.com/dictionary/vulnerable](https://www.merriam-webster.com/dictionary/vulnerable)

Also, if leaders present themselves to their team members as approachable, they will find out about abuse cases much more easily. This is because the vulnerable team members will be quicker to report the perpetrators.

**Figure 9: Harassment in the workplace.**

Coercive leadership power can also be used in such cases to ensure that the misbehavior is properly punished. However, if the type of harassment in question requires legal attention, appropriate measures should be taken to involve law enforcement as soon as possible.

## *Backgrounds*

Responsible leaders should realize their team members have different backgrounds and that not all those backgrounds had the same financial advantages. They should also remember that financial and social status often determine exposure to information and technology. This includes the schools that people can afford to attend, which further affects their capabilities due to the unequal availability of equipment and hands-on experience. People who attended better schools will often be more confident because most workplace equipment is not new to them. However, great leaders identify all potential, even when it is present in disadvantaged individuals. They nurture such individuals' abilities through in-depth orientation, monitoring, evaluation, and constructive feedback in order to build their confidence. At the same time, these effective leaders will also encourage other team members to come together and help their disadvantaged colleagues excel.

## *Grieving and Physical Unwellness*

When team members lose a loved one and are grieving, they may not be emotionally stable enough to handle the work given to them. The same applies to team members who may be physically unwell. It would be empathetic for a leader to allow these individuals to take some time off to rejuvenate themselves. I remember from my early career years, one of my supervisors sent flowers to my father's funeral, which was on a different continent from my workplace. I had never told him where the funeral would be held, yet he figured it out and took the initiative to send his condolences. While all examples don't have to be this extreme, it gives a real sense of belonging to be reminded that you work in a team where your supervisor genuinely cares about you.

The leader should note chronic conditions in their team members and identify ways to accommodate them without reducing the teams' productivity. For example, an asthmatic team member can be given tasks which do not expose them to dust. At the same time, their team members might be trained on where to find his or her inhaler and how to use it in the event of an attack. It is always beneficial for leaders to create a culture where team members look out for one another, which they can easily do through their natural influence.

## The Don'ts in Leadership Power

Sometimes leadership influence derives not from doing certain things, but from not doing them. And while some would argue that failing to do something is not an action, I say it is because it speaks volumes and produces results. In this section, we will explore how leadership power is exerted through "not doing," and what leaders can "not do" to inspire their teams and create a winning attitude.

### *Speaking Through Emotions*

We all get emotional sometimes, but managing your emotions is one of the most important things you can do for yourself and your team. For instance, you should never let your emotions speak for you. Instead, learn the art of collecting yourself and not speaking and making decisions while you are angry or upset. If possible, excuse yourself so that you can avoid getting emotional in the presence of your team members at all costs. Furthermore, you should never allow yourself to insult your team members, no matter what they have done. Remember, you are more than just a leader - you are a mentor, role model, pacesetter, counselor, you name it. Being unable to control your emotions is not something that you want to impact your team. In the end, emotional intelligence is a crucial tool.

## *Knowing it All*

Nobody knows everything. Or, as the old saying goes, "the only people who know everything are in the graveyard." Indeed, if you were to know everything, you could no longer learn anything, which would close the door to new ideas and innovation. So, seek advice, or at the very least, be open to it. Stop the "my way or the highway" attitude. Stop thinking that every communication should go from you toward others. Daniel Boorstin said, "The greatest enemy of knowledge is not ignorance, it is the illusion of knowledge.[66]" Be a wise leader and learn to learn from others.

## *Holding Grudges*

When you work with other people, conflicts are inevitable. Therefore, one of the competencies you need to develop as a leader is forgiving others and letting go of grudges. Holding grudges causes resentment, which is ultimately destructive to team unity. And once resentment grows in you as a leader, it will cause you to view everything your team members do through a negative lens. After that happens, it's unlikely that anything they do, no matter how innovative, will ever please you. In fact, your team members

---

[66] Boorstin, Daniel. *Knowledge Quotes (16 quotes).* Www.Goodreads.Com. https://www.goodreads.com/quotes/tag/knowledge

may eventually get frustrated and stop trying. Clearly, no winning team could blossom under such conditions, so learn to let go of your grudges and move on.

## *Delaying a Bit*

In Pablo Picasso's words, "only put off until tomorrow what you are willing to die having left undone.[67]" In terms of leadership, this means that you will not inspire your team with unfinished tasks that you keep postponing. After all, what creates your legacy is what you accomplish, not what's on your to-do list. At the same time, procrastinating only wastes time, which none of us has in unlimited quantities. So, once you have something planned, engage your team and get on it. Doing so gives your team the impression that you mean business, and – trust me - they will follow suit.

## *Eliminating "Thank Yous"*

The simple act of saying "thank you" can stop conflicts, increase enthusiasm, create a sense of acceptance, and a whole lot more. And contrary to what some people think, showing gratitude does not imply that you are weak or alter your status as a leader. It is as simple as showing appreciation for a job well done or acknowledging a persistent commendable performance. The way you feel about those words – the way you crave them when you know you've done a good job – is how your team members feel as

---

[67] *Picasso, P. (n.d.). A quote by Pablo Picasso. Www.Goodreads.Com.* *https://www.goodreads.com/quotes/27001-only-put-off-until-tomorrow-what-you-are-willing-to*

well. Try using "thank you" more often, and just see what happens to your team's morale and motivation.

## *Adopting the Blame Game*

One of the most challenging yet essential habits a leader must adopt is taking responsibility for mistakes and failures. Because while most leaders are more than happy to beat their chests for the accomplishments of the team (which is not recommended), they are quick to look for someone to blame in the face of mistakes and failures. However, playing the blame game does not encourage team spirit, nor is it an ingredient in the recipe for a winning culture.

## *Not Living up to Your Words*

When you take your own words for granted, your team members will do the same. For that reason, you must get in the habit of following up every word you say with an appropriate and timely action. If you say that the consequence of consistently missing deadlines is that pay raise will be withheld, stick to it. Even in negative instances, you'll ultimately gain the trust of your team by living up to your words. In the end, you cannot inspire a winning team when members are unsure whether or not your words will stand. In the end, they would always take some of your instructions for granted.

## *Heaping it on Yourself*

Do you aim to inspire your team? If so, you need to realize that delegation is critical in any winning team. When a leader fails to delegate, deadlines are missed, the leader is exhausted, and more mistakes are made. To make matters worse, team members don't learn anything. Without delegation, there is nothing to connect the leader to their team members because there is less to report on and, therefore, less on which to give feedback.

# Chapter 8: A Winning Culture Cultivating Tool

Leadership power is a potent tool for cultivating a winning culture in a team. However, there are conditions involved. That is to say - there are ways to direct one's power to accomplish the task. Of course, some of my recommendations for doing so have already been addressed in other chapters. In this chapter, we'll discuss the importance of listening and investing in a relationship. Specifically, we'll talk about why these factors are essential in steering one's leadership power toward winning.

## A Culture of Mindful Listening

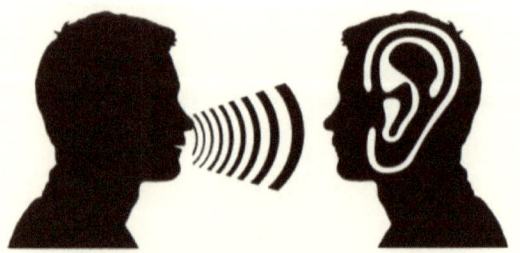

Figure 10: Listening is more than simply hearing.

People often mistake hearing for listening, but the two are not the same, nor are their results. After all, one does not *decide* to hear. Instead, whenever there are sounds around, they will be identified by the ear as vibrations, which are then converted to nerve impulses. These nerve impulses are then taken to the brain and translated into sounds. There is no effort on the part of the hearer taking place at any point in this process. Conversely, listening includes additional steps. It is also non-mandatory, meaning that you must actually expend effort to listen. To that point, a leader who adopts mindful listening is a lot closer to creating a winning culture.

## *Why Listening is Necessary*

Most leaders are used to talking, not listening. Just by looking at the two, one can deduce that talking is more active and result-oriented than listening, which is the primary reason leaders tend toward it. However, I invite you to try listening and thank me later. Below, I'll outline a few reasons why you should adopt listening as an essential aspect of your team's communication.

### You Get the Message

When a leader decides not to listen to their team members, they risk not receiving the message. When the sender's message does not reach the receiver, the result is a communication breakdown. This means you will be unable to act on their information. Should you choose to do so anyway, you are highly likely to act amiss.

### You Acquire Ideas

Ideas conveyed through talking are acquired through listening. These include new or better ideas that come from team members, colleagues, and supervisors.

### It's the Currency to Buy Loyalty

Listening is viewed as a commitment because it takes time and effort. Therefore, when you listen to your team members, they will feel cared for and accommodated. This makes them more engaged, respected, and appreciated.

### It Cultivates Team Spirit

Listening is an art that creates and sustains good relationships, even between leaders and team members. As we all know, good relationships are the primary ingredients for effective teamwork.

## *Categories of Listeners*

Listeners fall into five categories based on what they value most when they listen. As we highlight each one, you will undoubtedly note that some of them are situational, and some can be used in combination with others. I suggest you identify which category you fall into quickly. After that, try to find out if there are any adjustments you can make to help create a more winning environment for your team.

### "Who is Talking?" Listeners

This category of listeners is aligned toward understanding *who* is talking to them. Most of the time, their questions are about the communicator, not the message being conveyed. People-aligned listeners might be silently asking questions when someone is talking, such as "oh, I guess he likes striped ties? Last time I saw him, he was wearing another striped one," or thinking wandered thoughts like "he's built like a football player. Could he be a fan of Texans?" These listeners are considered "day-dreamers" because they are rarely focused on the communication being made.[68]

These listeners are far less likely to hear the details of the message because they are far too busy questioning and daydreaming. For that reason, we can categorize them as "hearers," not listeners. However, I prefer to call them "light listeners" instead. In some cases, people people-oriented listening can be a forerunner for other types of listening, with only the first few moments of communication being relegated to evaluating the speaker. These include cases where a listener might think, "she looks presentable," before moving on to real listening.

**"What Are You Talking About?" Listeners**

These listeners are mostly concerned with the content of the message being conveyed by the communicator. For this reason, they want to attach meaning to the message. This can include attempting to assess whether the message is accurate or not. To this category of listeners, detail is everything. Simply saying, "Spider silk is stronger than steel" is not enough for content-oriented listeners. They want to know where you got the information, why you think it's true, and will want evidence to support the statement. Content-oriented listeners need speakers who are well-

---

[68] Kelleher-Flight, B. (2012). *The essentials of active listening.* https://gdpconsulting.ca/wp-content/uploads/2014/08/the-essentials-of-active-listening.pdf

versed in what they have to say because they are highly attentive and usually ask follow-up questions.

## "What Do You Want?" Listeners

This category of listener dwells on the aim of the message. They want to know why the speaker is communicating the message in the first place so they can interpret the action required.[69] What does the speaker want? Do they need money, time, effort - what? Once these action-oriented or "task-oriented" listeners grasp the action required by the communicator, listening through further details (such as descriptions and explanations) will be very difficult for them.

## "When Are You Going to Finish?" Listeners

The main concern of these listeners is *time*. They either do not have much time to listen, or they have a short attention span. Therefore, they want messages that do not go around in circles but instead get straight to the point. Also, anything in the speaker's presentation that is somehow associated with time will be of serious concern to these listeners. For example, slow or staggered speech may quickly drain their patience. They may even convey their impatience through non-verbal communication like checking the time on their phone, rolling eyes, or fidgeting in their seats.

---

[69] Wrench, J. S. (2018, January 14). *The importance of listening in effective communication*. Brewminate.Com. https://brewminate.com/the-importance-of-listening-in-effective-communication

### "What Is the Message Beyond Your Words?" Listeners

This category of listeners is exceedingly rare, but teams must understand that they do exist. The category refers to listeners whose hearing goes far beyond the words of the communicator. They connect to the person talking and derive deep meaning that they feel is not directly conveyed in their words. This fact makes this type of listening a must-have tool for leaders who want to present themselves as mentors, counselors, and role models while assuming parental roles. As one might expect, empathy is an undeniably important factor for any leader who wants to acquire this ability.

When I was doing my MBA at Cornell University, I had a professor who was mentoring me. Deep down, I wanted to be an entrepreneur, but I simply didn't know how to go about it. However, since my desires were not within the project's scope, I never mentioned it to my mentor. Still, somehow, he noticed. In some way, he was able to see through me and hear beyond my words. One day, he said to me, "I don't want you to just think of earning an MBA, I want you to think about entrepreneurship." This really got to me and created an elevated resolve inside me - not only to work toward entrepreneurship but also to work under my mentor. When a leader sees beyond the words of their team members, they provide assurance that they care, something the other types of listeners may not be able to do.

## *The Recipe for Mindful Listening*

Listening is not as simple as it sounds. There are some things that need to be considered should it be mindful, or as others would prefer to call it "active.[70]" We will discuss some examples in the following section.

## It Begins with Hearing

Every listening process begins with the willingness to hear what someone has to say. For that reason, some of the steps that follow will be dependent on what and how you hear in the first place. For example, we can only remember what we have first heard. However, as you commit to hearing the speaker, remember not to start evaluating and judging just yet. The heart of the communication is yet to begin.

## My Ears Are All Yours

Showing that you are listening is crucial. It gives the speaker the confidence to continue speaking and encourages them to be honest. Additionally, it helps you to gain their trust.

For this reason, you should avoid disruptions such as cellphones or computer screens and make eye contact with the speaker. This will go a long way toward showing them that you're listening.

## Formative Response

The feedback you give your team members when speaking is called a formative response, and this too helps demonstrate that you are

---

[70] Wrench, J. S. (2018, January 14). *The importance of listening in effective communication*. Brewminate.Com. https://brewminate.com/the-importance-of-listening-in-effective-communication

listening. Examples of formative response include nodding your head, maintaining eye contact, and smiling. When necessary, ask relevant and appropriate questions for clarification. This also shows that you are really hearing what they're saying.

## Don't Accelerate the Pace

Once you decide to listen, you must remain patient. This not only means not interrupting your team members while they're speaking, but also not speaking for them during intermittent periods of silence. Let them do the talking and try to hear beyond their words during those short silences.

## Summary Response

A summary response comes at the end of the talk. This is when you should address the issue at hand through your feedback. At this point, you can either evaluate the message or request more time. You should also clarify any ideas, suggestions, and further questions you have on the message. In the end, your goal is to make sure that your team member is satisfied with your response.

## Fostering Connectivity and Human Relationships

There is something I have seen to be amiss in this world. For one, when people say that you should create meaningful relationships, they usually mean relationships with higher social, academic, career, or financial ranks. But if relationships with lower pay grade are not meaningful, what makes you think that someone on a higher pay grade should accommodate you when your pay grade is also lower than theirs? Therefore, the meaning in relationships is not measured by pay grades but by what we invest in those relationships. You see, relationships that are invested in always yield meaningful results, so it should be part of a leader's responsibility to invest in fostering meaningful relationships with their team members. This, however, does not necessarily mean all team members will be the best of friends.[71] Instead, they should develop a culture of respect without crossing personal boundaries. So, how can a leader foster connectivity with their team members? Let's explore.

## *Celebrate Life Beyond Work*

Life events such as marriages, anniversaries, births, birthdays, and buying a home are all part of life beyond work. Taking note and arranging celebrations for such events goes a long way toward fostering meaningful relationships. Surely, team members who have received such thoughtful attention cannot feel out of place. Still, the culture of celebrating milestones only works well if consistency is maintained. It can be disastrous if others note that others' milestones are celebrated while theirs seem to go unnoticed.

## *Use Technology*

Imagine what life could have been like during the COVD-19 pandemic without technology—no phones, WhatsApp, LinkedIn, Zoom, emails, you name it. It could have brought the world to a

---

[71] Achor, S. (2017, July 12). *How to foster social connections at work. Success.* https://www.success.com/how-to-foster-social-connections-at-work/

complete standstill. To that point, a modern leader uses technology to foster relationships with their team members. This means you should connect on LinkedIn, organize zoom meetings, and make friends on Facebook whenever possible. As an added benefit, introverted team members will find it easier to come out of their cocoons in virtual settings. Keep connected—it's essential for the success of your team.

## *Engage Frequently*

Like I said before, the little things matter. Just a simple smile and "Hello" when you see your team members can be very beneficial. And though some leaders think it denigrating to be the one to greet a team member, this is simply not true. Even worse, I've seen some leaders choose to keep quiet or just nod when greeted by their team members, which is a great way to quickly destroy a relationship. You simply cannot foster a winning culture that way. I suggest you hold short, frequent meetings with all of your team members - just to keep in touch. You might also consider chipping in and working with them when necessary. I promise you will never regret the investment.

## *Accommodate New Team Members*

Imagine being able to make a new team member feel at home even before their starting day. What an incentive you would be giving them to put their all into their new job. This is the sort of culture every leader should strive to create. After all, there is no harm in giving newcomers a quick phone call and telling them you are just checking in on them. It might seem awkward to them at first, but when the new hire meets you, they will be reassured that your interest was genuine. Moreover, you will have just made another future leader who will carry on that tradition.

## *Encourage Interpersonal Relationships Among Team Members*

Relationships in the team should not only be between the leader and the team members. The leader should also encourage team members to build relationships between themselves. Moreover, you should encourage them to know what is behind each team member - that is, the person beyond the role. This helps them to be on the lookout for each other, which is characteristic of "oneness." That said, people should not be pressured to go beyond their personal boundaries.

## *Encourage Relationships Beyond Team Boundaries*

Many advantages come with creating relationships with other teams rather than just your direct reports. For instance, ideas can be borrowed, network capital can be increased, and the chances of collaboration can be amplified.

# Chapter 9: Self-Awareness for Leaders

Just pose the question to a group: "how many of you are self-aware?" I bet you will see three-quarters if not all hands shoot up immediately. This is because most people truly believe they are self-aware, leaders included. But regardless of what we believe, a study by Tasha Eurich (2018) showed that only 10-15% of people are authentically self-aware - the rest just "think" they are. I know you are now wondering if you are part of the self-aware group. Not to worry - there's no harm in going through the self-awareness journey again and again, until you truly find yourself. But where do you start?

## What is Self-Awareness?

Self-awareness is a broad term, which is why there are multiple definitions of it. Some sources define self-awareness as a non-permanent moment of self-realization. Others describe it as the ability to differentiate between how we perceive ourselves and how others perceive us. You might also explain this as the ability to keep track of what happens in the world within ourselves, not the one outside us.[72] However, by combining these definitions, we can see

---

[72] Eurich, T. (2018, April 23). *What self-awareness really is (and how to cultivate it)*. Harvard Business Review. https://hbr.org/2018/01/what-self-awareness-really-is-and-how-to-cultivate-it

self-awareness as the conscious evaluation of oneself, which aims to authentically identify who one is. This involves discovering one's emotions, values, thoughts, strengths, and weaknesses.

Simply put, I perceive self-awareness as a "naming game" – one wherein an individual is named according to who they truly are. Self-awareness can take on two major dimensions, which we will describe in this section.

## *Who Am I?*

This form of self-awareness defines how you perceive yourself. Some call this "internal self-awareness," and it stipulates how you see your values, desires, aspirations, strengths, and weaknesses. It describes you against the standards of what you think you are capable of and explores what makes you feel either frustrated or proud. The former means that you would not have performed up to your standards, while the latter means that you would have surpassed them.

## *Who Do They Say I Am?*

This is also known as external self-awareness, and refers to the type of person other people say you are. These people could be friends, family, colleagues at work, those who attend church with you, or more importantly, your team members. What others say about you offers you a reflection of what they see in you and can help you better identify who you are. However, this only works if you are ready to accept that feedback in good faith.

## Is Self-Awareness Important?

Self-awareness is of paramount importance, especially to leaders. Yet, most leaders are averse to sharing their strengths and weaknesses with peers and receiving feedback from them. These leaders think doing so will damage their reputation, but in reality, peer feedback is critical to improving it. Remember, recognizing our personality and team member's personalities make things much easier in a team environment.

### *Effective Communication*

The betterment of relationships with team members, colleagues, and supervisors is enhanced by efforts to know oneself. Ultimately, a leader who is self-aware understands their emotions and can therefore manage them in a healthier way.[73] At the same time, improved emotional intelligence helps them better manage conflicts, which are inevitable whenever people work together. Self-aware leaders know how to communicate with their team members in ways that do not belittle their confidence. Furthermore, if the self-awareness sprouted from team member perceptions, the leader is more likely to develop a sense of empathy, which is healthy in all relationships.

---

[73] Forsey, C. (2018). *The true meaning of self-awareness (and how to tell if you're actually self-aware)*. Hubspot.Com. *https://blog.hubspot.com/marketing/self-awareness*

## *Presents Opportunity for Better Performance*

Self-awareness comes with the realization of the good, bad, and even the worst descriptions of yourself. When a leader understands their thoughts, behaviors, strengths, and weaknesses, they can identify where and what they need to improve. Indeed, acknowledging what you need to get better at is one of the first steps toward being your best self. This implies improved performance in all endeavors, including work, which can open the door to more promotions.

## *Stress Reduction*

Some of the stress we all suffer from is the result of little to no self-awareness. This is because many people waste time trying to be what they are not and engage in tasks they could never accomplish. For example, there are some tasks that are better performed by people whose personalities are more outgoing. If a person with a less outgoing personality were to try it, they would likely require much more effort to accomplish it. As you can see, true self-awareness reduces the chances of such frustrations, as one knows of what they are capable, and of what they are not.

## *Better Decision-Making Abilities*

The decision-making prowess of a self-aware leader is commendable. This could be because of improved confidence, as one knows what they can and cannot do. It could also be a factor of improved relationships, which help the leader make more well-informed decisions. That said, team members - who sometimes have information relevant to certain decisions - may find it hard to open up to a leader with whom they have an unhealthy relationship.

## *A Tool for Self-Control*

Self-control is a vital characteristic for successful leaders who lead winning teams. Usually, self-control sprouts from emotional intelligence, one of the critical benefits of self-awareness. This means that the leader becomes aware of their emotions in such a way that they can control them effectively, exhibiting good and exemplary leadership in the process. After all, you cannot control what you do not know, so self-awareness is a relevant tool for self-control.

## Types of Self-Awareness Tests

The need for self-aware leaders is constantly growing. This has also led to the development of tests for assisting this important assessment. These tests are known as self-awareness tests, and there are numerous available types. In this section, I will take you through some of these tests to ensure you understand what they are, how they work, and how to take them.

### *Mayer Salovey Caruso Emotional Intelligence Test (MSCEIT)*

The MSCEIT is a self-awareness test for emotional intelligence. According to this test, emotional intelligence evaluates how individuals acknowledge, use, understand, and manage their emotions.[74] This test is particularly important for helping leaders measure the extent to which they can solve emotional problems. It is taken by answering many non-partisan questions and responding to creative tasks designed to reveal a person's emotional stability.

After completing the test, a score is given to determine an individual's level of intelligence.

## *Myers and Briggs Personality Test*

The Myers and Briggs Types Indicator (MBTI) is a common personality test for enhancing self-awareness. In this test, personalities are defined based on the preferences of individuals to four pairs of parameters. These parameters are designated by letter abbreviations, which are used to determine an individual's overall personality. So that you can understand how they work, it's necessary to explain these parameter pairs in detail. However, as you go through the parameters, you will likely note some overlaps, but the one that describes you the most is the one that describes you the best.

### Sensing (S) or Intuition (N)

Sensing and intuition are parameters that explain how individuals gather and process information from their environment.[75]

---

[74] Mayer, J. D., Salovey, P., & Caruso, D. R. (2002). *Mayer-Salovey-Caruso emotional intelligence test (MSCEIT)*. Mhs.

[75] Kroeger, O., & Thuesen, J. M. (1988). *Type Talk : The 16 Personality Types That Determine How We Live, Love, and Work*. Dell Publications.

Individuals who are sensors prefer facts and specific responses to straightforward questions. For example, a sensor will prefer a straightforward answer to the question, "How much money are you left with?" This means the response should be presented as a figure. They are also fond of clarity and find satisfaction in tangible results.

On the other hand, intuitive people are less specific. They search for the deeper meaning hidden behind things. To answer the question, "How much money are you left with?" an intuitive person would probably say, "Enough to buy a burger," and that is more like a range because the prices for burgers could differ. Additionally, intuitive people find it difficult to concentrate on one thing, as they can be thinking of various things in any one moment.

## Thinking (T) or Feeling (F)

The Myers and Briggs theory suggests that humans make decisions based on information they gather through sensing or intuition. The decision-making process, however, is done by either thinking or feeling. In this case, thinkers are more fact-oriented than people-oriented. They favor making decisions based on facts and fairness, even if it would leave someone hurting. Generally, thinkers are objective and strong-willed individuals. Feelers are gentle-hearted and make decisions by considering the feelings of all the people involved – sometimes to the extent that they neglect themselves. In argumentative situations, feelers would choose peace over clarity. They are also rarely eager to prove a point.

## Extraversion (E) or Introversion (I)

Extraversion and introversion describe the extent to which individuals are externally or internally oriented. According to Kroeger and Thuesen (1988), whether one is introverted or extroverted is a matter of how and where they perform the functions of gathering and processing information and then using that information to make decisions. Extraverts find it easy to connect with anyone, even during their first encounters. They tend to prefer group rather than personal work, talking rather than listening, and talking first over thinking first. However, introverts mostly gather information with their eyes rather than their mouth. If they should say something, they will usually rehearse it first and are thus agitated by any interruption when they express themselves. Introverts find pleasure in spending time alone, and most of them are excellent listeners.

## Judging (J) and Perceiving (P)

Judging and perceiving express the life orientation of individuals - that is, the overall way they prefer to do things. In a nutshell, judges prefer step-by-step and timely methods of doing things, while perceivers only care about the end result and are more random in their approach. Individuals who subscribe to the "judging" preference are characterized as finding comfort in neatness, following specific schedules, and accomplishing tasks within specified timeframes. These individuals are focused and organized in their approach to life in general. But perceivers struggle to focus. As a result, they are the last-minute worker bees. After all, planning tasks is usually a wasted effort to them. These individuals care less about being orderly, and unlike their judging counterparts who find discomfort in surprises, perceivers are always happy to try new things.

**Analyzing Results**

Having gone through the parameter pairs, I am sure you have already identified the preferences that describe you best. After taking the test, you will be presented those preferences in the form of a four-letter abbreviated result. You then compare this result with an already-available list of sixteen (16) personality types. Let's take an example of someone who was determined to be intuitive, sensing, feeling, and judging, abbreviated as ISFJ. Comparing this with the Myers-Briggs list of personality identification will show that the individual is a "defender." Such an identification helps by bringing to light the strengths and weaknesses common to the defender personality type, making one understand themselves better. For instance, defenders are observant, enthusiastic, hardworking, and long-suffering, and these are some of their strengths. Some of their weaknesses are hiding their feelings, lack of flexibility when it comes to change, being hard on themselves, and overloading themselves.[76]

## *The Clifton Strengthsfinder Test*

The Clifton Strengthsfinder Test, also known simply as the Strengthsfinder test, was developed by Donald Clifton and his

---

[76] *NERIS Analytics Limited. (2013, August). Defender personality: Strengths and weaknesses. 16Personalities; NERIS Analytics Limited.*
*https://www.16personalities.com/isfj-strengths-and-weaknesses*

colleagues. It is based upon the principle of measuring talents and works by shifting concentration away from one's weaknesses. The idea is that more confidence and accomplishment are found when people realize their unique positive capabilities. The resulting awareness of one's strengths can then be a valuable tool for ensuring the best application of their abilities. For leaders, the importance of this cannot be overstated. After all, a leader who is aware of their strengths can better relate with team members and can properly focus on creating a winning team.

In the Clifton Strengthsfinder Test, there is a list of 177 pairs of sentences with prospective descriptions of oneself. I will give an example of two possible sentences which were given by Freeburg (2014): "I dream about the future" against "People are my great ally." In the exercise, you will be expected to choose the sentence that describes you better than the other one. You are given 20 seconds to choose your answer, after which the platform switches to the next pair of descriptions. Missing some questions is not a big deal unless you miss so many of them so that the assessment restarts.

## Analyzing Results

Upon completing the assessment, you will receive the test results in the form of well-ranked top-five signature themes. Individual results that define your theme print fingerprint will also be part of the results you get.[77]

---

[77] Freeburg, N. (2014, May 20). *What is the Clifton StrengthsFinder? Leadership Vision.* https://www.leadershipvisionconsulting.com/what-is-the-clifton-strengthsfinder/

Once you have a better idea of your strengths, you can take advantage of them when applying your leadership power.

## *360 Review*

This review is a form of professional feedback in which colleagues assess one another with respect to performance, competence, and contributions. The nomenclature of the 360 Review derives meaning from the number of degrees in a complete circle. This means that the feedback comes from all angles of the organization: peers, team members, other leaders, supervisors, and even customers. This information is gathered through various methods, including surveys, which are administered by external consultants. Digital instruments which give the results in the form of score are also sometimes used.[78]

## *DISC Personality Type*

DISC is an abbreviation for dominance, influence, steadiness, and conscientiousness, which are personality traits created by William Moulton Marston. This personality type test determines the personality of an individual based on these four parameters by forcing them to choose the one or two that suit them best. This results in a personality standardized by the 12 possible parameter combinations.

---

[78] Heathfield, S. M. (2020). *You can obtain feedback for performance improvement using 360 Reviews*. The Balance Careers. https://www.thebalancecareers.com/what-is-a-360-review-1917541

## Analyzing Results

According to the DISC test, an individual's single or paired choices of parameters can be matched with descriptions of that person's personality. For instance, if you choose D (dominance) and C (conscientiousness), the matching personality type is "challenger," which is designated as DC. According to this test, a "challenger" is a person who is focused, extremely organized, independent, and outspoken.[79] Contrarily, "D" on its own represents a "winner" personality type.

## *Social Styles Model*

Developed by David Merill and Roger Reid, the Social Styles Model is an assessment that helps individuals pinpoint their preferences on social styles and communication.[80] This is done by analyzing both their responsiveness and assertiveness.[81] Assertiveness is analyzed based on the methods the subjects apply when being assertive - that is, whether they ask or tell.

---

[79] Cole, G. J. (2018, May 14). *How to recognize which DISC personality type you are.* Truity. *https://www.truity.com/blog/how-recognize-which-disc-personality-type-you-are*

[80] Clayton, M. (2017, April 18). *David Merrill & Roger Reid: Social styles.* Management Pocketbooks. *https://www.pocketbook.co.uk/blog/2017/04/18/david-merrill-roger-reid-social-styles/*

[81] de Beer, L. (2019, May 23). *Conflict management 102 – The four social styles and mastering personality differences.* Legadima. *https://legadima.co.za/conflict-management-social-styles/*

Responsiveness is perceived as how the subjects prefer to manage their emotions, either by controlling or displaying them.

**Analyzing Results**

Depending on the paired preferences on both assertiveness and responsiveness, there are four sets of results for the Social Styles Model. If an individual prefers assertiveness by asking and responsiveness by controlling emotions, they are tagged as "analytical." On the other hand, one who prefers assertiveness by telling and responsiveness by displaying emotions is described as "expressive." The other remaining social styles are "driving" and "amicable."

## *Leadership Continuum Theory*

Tannebaum and Schmidt are the brains behind the development of the Leadership Continuum Theory, which subscribes to the notion that most classifications of leadership are extreme, including democratic and autocratic leadership styles. For that reason, the leadership continuum theory settles for the idea that, realistically, leadership styles lie somewhere in the range between these classifications. Therefore, it helps leaders become aware of the types of leaders that they are, based on how they make decisions under the influence of three pressures. These pressures are situational pressure, the leader's inner pressure, and pressure that emanates from the team members.[82]

---

[82] Scouller, J., & Chapman, A. (2011). Tannenbaum and Schmidt's leadership behaviour continuum - BusinessBalls.com. Businessballs.Com.

## Analyzing Results

The theory separates leaders into seven categories, arranged from left to right, depending on their methods of making decisions. At the far left, the leader retains all the power to make decisions. These "tell leaders" do not include their team members in the decision-making process at all. If the team members are told to jump, they are expected to only ask, "how high?" As we move toward the right of the continuum, the leader will give more and more decision-making control over team members. At the far-right, team members can make their decisions without any interference from the leader at all.

## *The Big Five Personality Model*

Also acronymized as the "O.C.E.A.N." or "C.A.N.O.E." model, the Big Five Personality Model is a self-awareness test that defines an individual's preferences based on five major traits: conscientiousness, agreeableness, neuroticism, openness, and extraversion.[83] Other self-awareness tests classify individuals into inflexible paired traits, such as introversion and extraversion. The Big Five Model is built on the notion that individuals are usually in-between these two extreme traits. For that reason, it is designed to measure the level to which one is oriented toward one or the other. For instance, the Big Five Model measures the extent to

---

*https://www.businessballs.com/leadership-models/leadership-behaviour-continuum-tannenbaum-and-schmidt/*

[83] *Lim, A. G. Y. (2020). Big Five Personality Traits | Simply Psychology.* https://www.simplypsychology.org/big-five-personality.html

which an individual is extraverted, rather than categorizing them as either introverted or extroverted. It has been reported that the Big Five traits are factors of genetic and environmental influence, and their heritability is approximately 50%.

## Conscientiousness

Conscientiousness refers to the tendency of an individual to regulate their impulses in socially acceptable ways to engage in goal-oriented behaviors.[84] Some of the traits here are self-discipline, reliability, persistence, ambition, consistency, and hard work. In that regard, individuals who are high in conscientiousness are more persistent, consistent, reliable, ambitious, self-disciplined, and hard working. They do not seek immediate gratification at the expense of their long-term goals[85]

## Agreeableness

Agreeableness measures the extent to which one can relate well with others. Estimating factors such as trust, kindness, patience, sensitivity, and loyalty gives an idea of an individual's orientation toward others. Essentially, highly agreeable people are associated with higher levels of the traits just mentioned, while the opposite is also true.

---

[84] Ackerman, C. E. (2019, June 19). Big Five Personality Traits: The OCEAN model explained [2019 Upd.]. PositivePsychology.Com. https://positivepsychology.com/big-five-personality-theory/
[85] van Thiel, E. (2018). What are the Big Five Personality Test Traits? - Learn all about the theory. 123test.com. https://www.123test.com/big-five-personality-theory/

## Neuroticism

The overall emotional stability and temper of a person defines their neuroticism. Pessimism, jealousy, moodiness, self-criticism, fear, and nervousness are traits associated with high levels of this trait, with such individuals possessing an elevated self-conscience is elevated and being quick to anger. On the other hand, those whose scores are at the lower end of the "neuroticism continuum" tend to be far more confident and emotionally stable.

## Openness

Openness refers to one's readiness to engage in new things, including imaginative and intellectual ventures. People more open to new experiences are identified by their higher curiosity, creativity, imagination, preference for variety, and insightfulness compared to their less open counterparts.[13]

## Extraversion

The extent to which one desires or seeks to interact with their external environment, especially people, is referred to as extraversion.[12] In addition to reflecting the level at which an individual is assertive, extraversion also defines where an individual derives their energy. This is because people who derive more energy from their internal environment - that is, from within themselves - are regarded as less extroverted than those who recharge themselves through their external environment. Some of the factors that define extraversion are talkativeness, social confidence, and an outgoing nature.[13]

## Analyzing the Results

In the Big Five Personality Model, personalities are determined according to the Big Five Inventory, which Goldberg developed in 1993. The inventory consists of 44 items related to the five major aspects of the Big Five Model. An individual's responses to the 44 items are summarized to obtain a score for each aspect, such as agreeableness or conscientiousness. This score then determines the level to which one is oriented toward a particular trait.

# Conclusion

Remember, power controls while leadership influences. Leadership, coupled with power, yields leadership power, which should, in turn, be controlled by all of the good qualities of leadership. If not abused knowingly or through ignorance, leadership power is a potent tool for building a winning culture. Through it, teams can make winning a reality, not just a dream.

In this book, I identified two major aspects as key to a leader's ability to inspire their team, create a winning culture, and lead to win. These are task-orientation and people-orientation. In addition to these, the action of "stopping some things" is a unique angle of positively using leadership power to impact team success.

## Task Orientation

Unwavering focus on the successful completion of the team's tasks is a must-have attribute in all leaders who aspire to lead to win. This entails good planning, the correct delegation of duties among team members, efficient communication, and frequent progress and performance evaluations, among other factors.

### *Attention to Motives*

Tasks are best accomplished when the leader sets the right motives at the beginning of the tasks. In such cases, well-set motives are good enough encouragement for leaders and their teams to accomplish their goals. Well-communicated motives can transform the leader's motive into the team's motive, which is an important step in creating a winning team. It makes it far more likely that the leader and team members will see the goal through the same lens.

Leaders should also be aware that their team members have their own motives, some of which negatively impact the productivity of the team if they are not attended to. These motives could be social, physiological, or personal. Still, team goals work best when they accommodate the goals of individual team members. Although this sounds like an impossible mission, it can accommodate the more obvious motives like the acquisition, hunger, and thirst motives, which require one attend to the timely and fair compensation of team members.

## *Embracing Challenges*

Even with the most effective planning, challenges are inevitable. However, a leader who throws a tantrum at the sight of a challenge creates a team of quitters, not winners. We become more experienced in this life through the challenges we encounter in our endeavors to accomplish certain goals. After all, there is no point in calling yourself and your team "winners" when there has never been something to contend within the first place. Simply put: winning is not in avoiding challenges but in conquering the challenges you face.

## *Adopt Proactivity*

Procrastination is the enemy of proactivity. Putting off tasks creates last-minute scenarios, which are often accompanied by even more mistakes and mishaps. On the other hand, proactivity gives the leader more control over things that might be unplanned. At the same time, completing tasks as planned demonstrates the leader's focus on achieving goals - an attribute that can be easily adopted by their team members.

## People Orientation

Leadership power has a much more positive impact when it upholds the sanctity of humanity. As teams achieve their set goals, meaningful human relationships should also be nurtured, along with other humane traits such as empathy.

### *Personalities*

Personalities are indispensable as far as the influence of leadership power is concerned. Indeed, a leader's ability to identify their personalities and those of their team members, colleagues, and supervisors can help them manage these personalities in ways that create a winning culture in their teams. Furthermore, some tasks are better performed by certain personalities, and leaders can adapt better communication and conflict resolution when they are aware of the different personalities surrounding them. In the end, the impact of personalities on leadership power is unignorable because personalities are interrelated with other aspects that affect leadership power, such as leadership styles.

## *Listening Beyond Words*

Although many types of listening address different situations, listening beyond words can yield amazing results and foster mutual understanding in teams. Listening beyond words achieves the primary purpose of listening to an elevated extent, because it does not just seek the message from the words being spoken, but from the factors contributing to them.

## *Caring for the Disadvantaged and Vulnerable*

Leaders can apply leadership power to address issues of conscious and unconscious gender discrimination. In hiring, it is recommended that leaders scout for prospective team members based on their abilities, not on their gender affiliations. It is also appropriate that all gender affiliations be accommodated in teams. If leaders instill this culture in their team members, it is more likely the team members will look out for each other, irrespective of their gender. Appropriately-utilized leadership power can serve as a weapon against the harassment of the vulnerable in the workplace. However, leaders can also misuse their power to promote harassment. Such misuse of leadership power only fosters an environment of fear and insecurity. Ultimately, a winning culture cannot grow out of such an environment.

## The Action in "Not Doing"

The influence of leadership power is not only in doing some things but in "not doing" others. Of course, learning and adopting what needs to be refrained from is as important as learning and adopting what needs to be done. Some of the things a leader should look out for include being ungrateful, building resentment through keeping grudges, blaming others for mishaps and failures, unleashing emotions in front of team members, not living up to their words, and displaying an unwillingness to work with others.

However, leaders should not be focused solely on creating a winning culture in their teams, but creating the *right* winning culture. They should inspire their teams to aim at authentic winning, not manipulated winning. For instance, the right winning attitude does not accommodate bribery and ill-use of connection power just to hold the crown.

Whatever a leader decides to do or not do implies the type of future leaders they are creating, because every leader is likely to make multiple copies of themselves (whether they intend to or not).

Be honest with yourself and try to imagine the sort of leaders you are sending out into the world. Are they winners or failures? If your answer is the latter, now is the time to make changes.